THE OLD WILDERNESS ROAD

WILLIAM O. STEELE

THE OLD
WILDERNESS ROAD
An American Journey

Illustrated with maps

Harcourt, Brace & World, Inc., New York

TO HEATHCLIFF

mostly called Pig Dog; known hereabouts as Hero Dog.

IN MEMORY OF

his steadfast companionship along numerous mountain roads
and trails and his constant protection
from the dangers of moonshiners,
alligators, mud holes, and high cliffs.

Though he was a member of the family
in decisions and activities,
he never learned to handle a knife and fork and
sit at the family table.
Still, he sat high above the salt.

FARE-THEE-WELL, BULLDOG COMPANION!

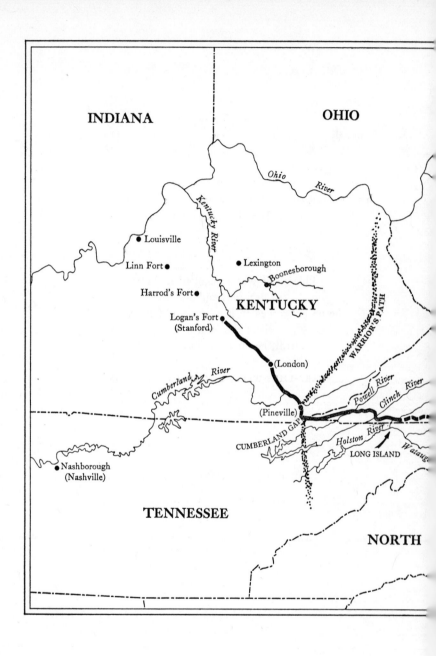

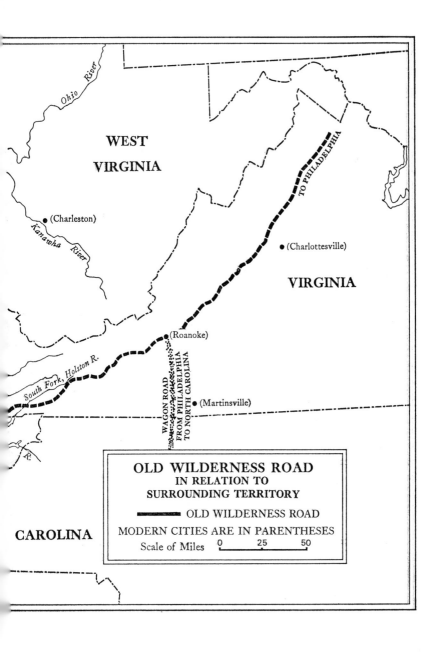

Ohio River

WEST
VIRGINIA

• (Charleston)

Kanawha River

TO PHILADELPHIA

• (Charlottesville)

VIRGINIA

•(Roanoke)

South Fork, Holston R.

WAGON ROAD
FROM PHILADELPHIA
TO NORTH CAROLINA

• (Martinsville)

R.

CAROLINA

OLD WILDERNESS ROAD
IN RELATION TO
SURROUNDING TERRITORY

━━━━ OLD WILDERNESS ROAD
MODERN CITIES ARE IN PARENTHESES
Scale of Miles   0   25   50

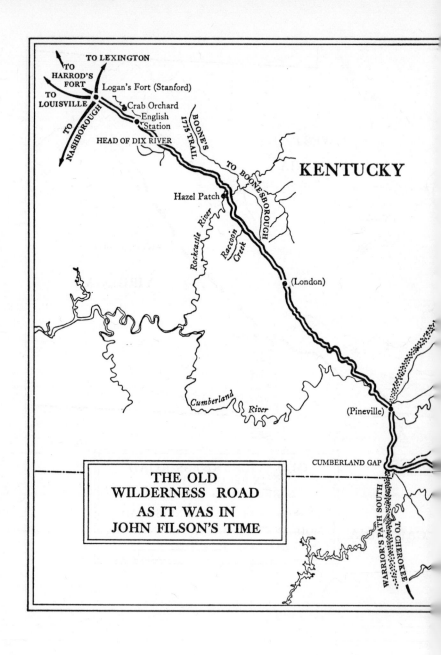

THE OLD
WILDERNESS ROAD
AS IT WAS IN
JOHN FILSON'S TIME

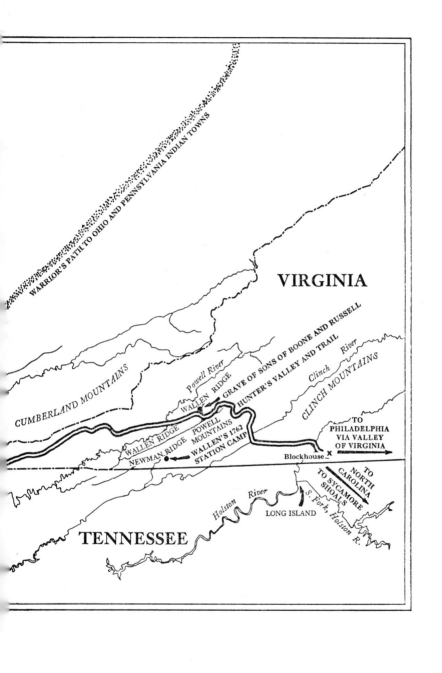

"The land was ours before we were the land's."
—from "The Gift Outright" by ROBERT FROST

CONTENTS

xi

INTRODUCTION

Out of the dimness of interior America, where huge bones of long-dead beasts cast awesome shadows; where caves breathed mysterious airs from the hollows of the earth; where salt springs flowed miraculously side by side with sweet limestone waters; where game animals stood in the meadows packed together so tight that sunlight could not get through to the ground—somewhere amidst this mixture of fact and tall tales, of the known and the unknown—was shaped the first state west of the Appalachian Mountains. It was Kentucky, the first finger of the new nation, a finger pointing westward, directing the future course for restless, always-on-the-move Americans to follow.

Before Harrodsburg, the first settlement, was begun in 1774, Kentucky was empty of Indians and white pioneers. Then it was a part of Virginia and referred to as the "back country" by those along the coast, who fronted toward and traded with Mother England. When Kentucky became the fifteenth state in 1792, it had over 70,000 inhabitants, many thriving towns, a college, and a newspaper—all this accomplished in only eighteen years. Suddenly attitudes, interests, and geography took a new direction. Stuck out in the wilderness two hundred

1

leap-frogging miles from the nearest older settlements, Kentuckians were at the front of an expanding nation, and *they* brazenly called the coastal dwellers and their towns the "back country." The pot was naming the kettle black.

Not only change and progress came to Kentucky in those eighteen years, but also the buckskinned hero, a folk figure born of the many fights with Indians on the "dark and bloody ground." With ax, rifle, and log cabin, he conquered the wilderness, defeated the Indians, and passed on into the American national character. From his lips came the harsh statement that sealed the Indian's fate: "A dead Injun is the only good Injun." He knew the horror of the war whoop and the slash of the scalping knife and felt justified in his belief.

Kentuckians had no inferiority complexes. These new-born Americans faced inland, westward, and their steps would lead to one frontier after another, on across the continent, the buckskinned heroes pulling a new, often reluctant, and unsure national government along with them. In eighteen short years, the frontier had assumed the shape that it would always have in fact and fiction and had developed its symbols for all times. It had become a powerful influence, and it was on the move.

And how had so much been accomplished so fast? Mostly by the energies of the frontier folks who walked into Kentucky with their woodlore, their keen-shooting long rifles, their plant knowledge, and their handicrafts; who poured into Kentucky with their hard and long-learned frontier know-how over the first and most rugged route across the Appalachian barrier—the Wilderness Road.

Although it was only a narrow trail that wound

through the mountain wilderness, it carried the name "road." Pioneers never used the word "trail" to denote their routes; they sometimes said "path," less often "trace," but mostly they called any single-track course a "road." The Wilderness Road would not become a road in the sense used today—wide enough for two-way traffic of wheeled vehicles—until 1795, when the Kentucky legislature appropriated money to make the route thirty feet wide to afford safe and easy passage for wagons and carriages. But it was too late then to serve much purpose for Kentucky. In spite of its new status, the Wilderness Road was already beginning to vanish by that time.

The road had many names, among them "the Road to Caintuck," "the Great Western Road," "the Kentucky Path," but the Wilderness Road seems the most appropriate, for that is what it was—a roadway through the wilderness. It is often difficult to pinpoint the exact beginning or ending of old trails and roads. Writers on the Wilderness Road have used many different eastern and western terminal places in telling of its history.

In this book the Wilderness Road will begin at the Blockhouse in Virginia. Here feeder paths came together, and here migrants waited for others heading for Kentucky. The more guns there were, the safer the traveling would be, for Indians lurked constantly along the road. The western terminus will be Logan's Station, Kentucky, for at that point paths spread out in many directions. Crab Orchard, eight miles east of Logan's, marked the end of the hardest going, but it was never as important a stopping place as Logan's Station. These two hundred miles from the Blockhouse to Logan's have rightly been called "the longest, blackest, hardest road of pioneer days in America."

There was another way to reach Kentucky, and that was by the Ohio River. It was not used as much as the Wilderness Road in the early days, for at that time few pioneers had experience with western river navigation. The dangers from unknown shoals, ice, and high water were much too frightening for most people to risk. But perhaps the one factor that made the Ohio route most unpopular was the outrageously high prices of boats and pilots in Pittsburgh. Money was too scarce and precious for settlers to waste it filling the pockets of profiteers in that Ohio River port. Also a good boat or pilot didn't keep away the northern Indians, who were always a threat anywhere or anytime along the winding Ohio.

A full accounting of the events and the travelers of the Wilderness Road would encompass too much, as would the complex story of the settling of Kentucky. So this volume is only minimally concerned with each. Mainly this is a glimpse of the road through the eyes of four persons who contributed to the linking of disconnected routes into one specific, historic route.

And if the day is especially clear and the reader's sight keen, perhaps it might just be that he will find himself standing in the middle of the road looking eastward back the long way to England, while to the west he might see that the road doesn't stop in Kentucky but that it winds on across the landscape to become the Western Movement, Manifest Destiny, the Great Migration, the American Civilization of bathroom plumbing, Cokes, computers, space programs. It is a breathless view, this great sweep of America, and I hope that every reader will see at least something of it from the Wilderness Road.

NEWSCAST OF 1749

A quick glance at a few important events
pertaining to Britain's largest and oldest American colony

QUESTION OF THE YEAR

In 1749 King George's War has only recently ended and
the inked signatures on the peace treaty between France
and England are hardly dry, yet already, as this year begins, there is talk of another war between the two powers. The north-south Appalachian Mountain chain in
North America separates the indefinite territorial claims
of the French in the interior from those of the coast-
hugging British colonies. But how long will this wild, unin-
habited wilderness barrier of high peaks and huge trees
and rocky rivers make a buffer between these two great
nations contending for the North American continent?
That is the question the French are asking themselves this
year as they keep an eye on mountain passes.

BURIED WORDS

The French are doing more than watching and worrying.
They are burying lead plates at strategic points along the
Ohio River. These contain inscriptions that proclaim the
Ohio and its tributaries belong to France by the right of
first discovery, of extensive exploration, and of signed
treaties with Great Britain.

Are the French mad to do such a thing or, perhaps, only superstitious? Do they consider the lead plates as talismans, wonder-working charms whose protective power will ward off the threatening British? Perhaps they reason that since peace between nations can be made by burying war hatchets, then the French-American interior can be kept safe by burying strong words of proclamation in the soil.

Will the lead plates prove effective? As the year advances, the answer to that question seems to lie with the oldest and largest of the North American British colonies. The destiny of North America might well depend on Virginia.

SEA-TO-SEA VIRGINIA

Virginia has always claimed by charter rights from the English king a vast territory extending from the Atlantic straight across the continent to the distant Pacific Ocean, and also from the western limits of Pennsylvania northwest to Lake Erie and from there westward. This has been assumed to be a sheer illusion of grandeur on Virginia's part, since little effort has been made to explore or control this vast western domain. Now, however, the picture is changing. Virginia's interest in what is termed "the land back of the settlements" is quickening. This is most significant, but why has it taken a century and a half since Jamestown for such ferment?

TIDEWATER VIRGINIA AT THE MERCY OF A VILLAIN

Since the days of their first colonization, Virginia settlers have generally considered themselves an outpost of the British Empire. As they pushed cautiously inland, they made their homes along the deep tidal rivers and so were able to keep and strengthen their ties with the mother country because each plantation had its own wharf and ocean-going ships were able to come directly from England to any particular plantation and unload their cargo. All the luxuries of life and even many of the necessities came from England. The planters' children embarked at their own docks for schooling in England; families left there to visit kin in the mother country or revel in the pleasures of the gay social life of London. The Virginians had little contact with the other British colonies in America. The Tidewater aristocrats seemed not to care what happened in Boston or in Charles Town and lived their easy-going lives modeled on the English country gentlemen.

Now, in this year of 1749, life along the tidal rivers goes grandly on as always, with dances in the plantation ballrooms, the men and women dressed in the latest London fashions. There are gatherings in the parlors to discuss the latest British books and magazines, to relate court gossip received on the latest merchant vessel. There are horse races and betting, card games and musicales. And, as always, work continues for the planters, as they manage their huge estates and keep their ledgers and account books up to date.

Still, underneath all this activity, there lurks an uneasiness, for many of the plantation owners are deeply in debt to British trading houses. There is little hope of payment since overproduction has resulted in tobacco of very poor quality, and prices have dropped. New Tidewater land for growing finer tobacco no longer exists. Libraries, mansions, racing stables, estates—all seem likely to have to be sold to meet the terrible debts. The Golden Age of Virginia Tidewater aristocracy has reached its peak, and the future holds little more than dire threats to their rank, their power, and their stylish manner of living.

Tobacco is the villain!

FROM "DIVINE TOBACCO" TO "THAT STINKING WEED"
Once tobacco was believed by the English to have miraculous healing power and was considered a divine plant. Then smoking became a novelty, next a fashion, and finally a custom necessary to vast numbers of peoples as the usage spread across Europe. This created a great demand for tobacco, and Virginians rushed in and took advantage of that demand, building their early colonial economy around this money crop. A large number of families made their fortunes in Virginia in the seventeenth century by raising tobacco and selling it in England. And as Tidewater wealth increased, so did the planters' power and influence till these newly rich bigwigs controlled the colony's affairs.

But tobacco requires the richest loam for the best growth, and it exhausts the soil very fast. Three or four crops and a field has to be abandoned for tobacco, though it is usable for other crops. This makes for constant clearing of new ground, which in turn requires a huge labor force of African slaves to accomplish. Little thought has been given to the time when all the unused land in the Tidewater region will be gone. Most planters have been far too busy packing the golden leaves into casks and keeping these rolling aboard the British merchant ships, and busy also buying slave after slave, to try to make more money with a steadily increasing work force.

Now, in 1749, however, many are calling tobacco "that stinking weed" and have given up raising it. These planters wonder what can take its place. What will support them in the grand manner to which they are accustomed? A few pin their hopes for future wealth on land—western land, the empty land back of the Piedmont and the Great Valley settlements, land belonging to Virginia by charter rights, land that the French might grab if Virginians don't act at once.

GET-RICH-QUICK COMPANIES

A land company works on the assumption it can be given, free of charge, unoccupied land that it will then sell for clear profit. Though little is known of the area west of the Virginia settlements, ignorance does not keep many prominent and powerful men of the colony from forming land companies to speculate on the unsettled land there. This year several companies petition the Virginia Council for huge tracts, and one million acres have been granted them in such general terms as "west of the Great Mountains" and "to the westward."

One of the most important groups asking for land is the Ohio Company, which has received 200,000 acres somewhere along the Ohio River in the region where the French have buried their lead plates of ownership. The company plans to send out someone to explore the area and later to erect a fort somewhere. Also a road will be built for the incoming settlers to use.

Another get-rich-quick company of Virginia has been granted 800,000 acres in an indefinite area west and north of the boundary line of North Carolina. It is the Loyal Company, and already as the year ends, one of its thirty-nine members has been selected to explore to the west and seek settlement sites. He is Thomas Walker of Albemarle County in the Piedmont country close to the Blue Ridge.

PART ONE
DOCTOR THOMAS WALKER
British Colonial—Half American

Needle in a Haystack

The dogs swirled under and around the saddled horses, snapping at each other and scuffling like young puppies. To one side sat an old hound, its body scarred, one long ear missing. It paid no heed to the other dogs.

A man came out of the house and crossed the yard with short, brisk steps. The dogs saw him and with excited yelps streamed toward him. He held his writing case and inkhorn over his head as they leaped against him, squirmed between his legs, and all but tripped him.

Thomas Walker, physician and master of the plantation, Castle Hill, laughed and waded spryly on through the pack to where his horse was tied. He shoved the writing paraphernalia into his saddlebag. Then he went over to the old hound and patted its head and rubbed the ear stump fondly. Two years ago the hound had accompanied him down the Great Valley of Virginia on a journey of exploration and had lost the ear in a terrible fight with a bear. Now Doctor Walker was taking the old dog into the wilderness with him again. In fact, he wouldn't go without such a valuable companion. And who knew what adventures the two of them might have this time?

With a final pat he moved away and began to notice

the other dogs, one by one, with a rub of a muzzle here and a tweak of a soft ear there, and with kind words for all. Several belonged to the men accompanying him on this journey, but these strangers sought his attention as much as did his own dogs.

A servant brought out a horse from the smithy and led it back and forth. Colby Chew and the Negro smith stood in the open doorway watching the animal's gait, for there was a new shoe on one forefoot. Ambrose Powell and William Tomlinson sauntered out of the smithy shed and began to check their riding gear. John Hughes came up, wrapping a flap of leather around his gunlock for protection. He tied the weapon to the bundle behind his saddle.

Walker looked inside the smithy. Four of the group he had picked to go with him into the wilderness were here, ready to leave. Where was the fifth? The party should be under way. He scanned the gray stippled sky. It would be raining by tomorrow for sure, perhaps this very afternoon. But riding in the rain was the least of his worries, for they might well face worse than dampness before this exploration was finished.

The doctor was a member of the Loyal Company of Virginia, which had employed him to search for good land behind the settled part of the colony. The company had official permission to take 800,000 acres of land somewhere to the west. Surveys by the company had to be completed in four years or the grant would be lost. But first this back country had to be explored, since it was not known how far westward the mountains extended or whether there was a route through them. And beyond the mountains—what kind of land lay there? Was it fertile, suitable for farming, tree-covered? Were there streams for grist mills? Were there lead mines, salt springs, or rocky wastes? What would the six of them find to the west where no Virginian had ever yet set foot?

A servant led up two packhorses. Their loads were light, for much remained to be picked up on the way. Behind them came Henry Lawless, the missing member of the party, feeling the fresh-ground edge of his ax with a thumb.

Everything was prepared to Walker's satisfaction, so he and his five companions mounted. The dogs ran about with yelps of pleasure, impatient to be gone. Mrs. Walker came out on the porch with Thomas, Junior, wrapped in a shawl in her arms. She called out farewells. The other three Walker children raced about their mother, waved and yelled, and swung around the porch posts wildly. The doctor shouted back at them. Then with one final good-by he rode off, the old dog trotting alongside. The other riders strung out behind, the last one leading the two pack animals.

It was the sixth of March, 1750, and Walker, who kept a brief journal of their travels, said they left at ten o'clock. The history of the Wilderness Road had begun and along with it the Westward Movement, which was eventually to change the strip of Atlantic colonies into a continental nation, independent and self-confident. Thomas Walker could hardly have been aware of such momentous events. If anyone had predicted such an outcome, he would likely have scoffed. He was a plain and simple man who hated pompous display and fancy ideas. He was going westward, for "a certain consideration," to look for a place for settlement. It was business, nothing more.

And it was a business that most probably caused him

some uneasiness as he rode southward across the Virginia Piedmont country. He knew the fickleness of the wilderness, the useless thrashing for days through laurel slicks, the exhausting climbs over rocky mountains. He was not a woodsman, not entirely at home in the wilderness in spite of his past experiences. He was aware that his exploration might well come to naught in the uncharted back country—unless . . . unless he found a way through the Appalachian Mountains. Indians told traders of a pass, but the red men had been known to lie. Was it there? And could he find it if it was—this needle in a haystack?

2

Interior America—
a Blank Piece of Paper

A few miles south of Walker's place lay Shadwell, the home of Peter Jefferson. The journal does not mention a stop here, but Jefferson was a very good friend, and Walker often visited Shadwell and played with young Thomas. Whatever Peter Jefferson knew about the back country Walker was sure to have long since found out, so there was little need to stop.

Jefferson had been one of the colony's surveyors extending the Virginia-North Carolina boundary line westward the year before. The other official surveyor with him had been his friend, Joshua Fry. The two had completed many surveys about the colony in recent years, and Fry, who held several important positions in Albemarle County, constantly furthered Jefferson's career by making him his assistant in official posts and projects. Fry and Jefferson were also members of the Loyal Company, and it was only natural that Walker spent the first night of his journey at Viewmont, Fry's home, several miles to the south of Shadwell.

Joshua Fry had been educated at Oxford. After his arrival in Virginia, he had been appointed Master of the Grammar School at William and Mary College in Wil-

liamsburg, the colony's capitol. Here he taught Indian
students as well as white ones. Later, he was Professor
of Philosophy and Mathematics at the college, but he quit
teaching to live in the Virginia Piedmont. Though his
home was in what he termed the back settlements, he
lived there by choice, he said, so as to "raise a fortune"
to support his family, something he had been unable to
accomplish on his teacher's salary at William and Mary
College in the Tidewater.

After supper that night at Viewmont, the Fry family
retired and Walker's companions went to their sleeping
quarters. Then Colonel Fry led Walker to a room whose
walls were lined with books. A servant followed with an
armload of wood and built up the fire. He placed candles
across the mantelpiece, lit them, and left.

Whether Fry considered this room a study or a library,
it was most evident that it was *his* workroom. There was
surveying equipment scattered everywhere; stacks of
books rested on chairs and were piled on the floor against
cabinets; and on and under benches were a variety of
tools and muddy boots and boxes of samples of dirt and
rocks. Walker laughed on entering the room. There
seemed as much confusion here as at his last visit. And
certainly this miscellaneous collection made him feel as
much at home as at Castle Hill among his own disarray
of fossils, dried plants, doctoring implements, medical
books, and a human skelton, partly assembled. Who had
time in the pressing world of 1750 to stop whirling long
enough to store away every item in a neat and tidy way?
Who indeed, when events were a-spawning and ideas fer-
menting.

Taking a long taper, Fry lighted it at the hearth and

then touched its flame to the wicks of four tall candles standing on a table. He pushed away papers on which were scrawled mathematical equations and geometrical figures and slid several maps from underneath them. He called Walker to his side, and in the brightness the two studied the map of North America, drawn by Daniel Coxe, and compared it to that by Herman Moll and one by Delisle. Fry discussed what Walker might hope to find to the westward and admitted that, though these maps represented the best geographical knowledge of the day, there was little enough of it, and that little was much too general in nature. Fry wanted information about the western regions for the map he and Jefferson had been commissioned to draw for the English Board of Trade, which also wanted an account of the boundaries of Virginia, as well as information on recent settlements and on all encroachments by foreigners on the colony's land.

Fry showed the doctor their uncompleted map of Virginia, pointing out how sparse was information about the west, how little there was to ink onto the white space between the Allegheny Mountains and the Mississippi River south of the Ohio River. Even the French had not named this region, yet they claimed it as their own.

He read aloud to Walker several passages from journals of French explorers and from those of missionaries, for he had an excellent collection of material about France and its conquest of interior America. When he had finished, Walker agreed with Fry that the French certainly were boastful in claiming so much territory, and both men felt that France had taken land to the west that was Virginia's by charter rights.

The cartographer went to a drawer and took out some

loose sheets of paper. It was the journal of John Peter
Salley, who left Virginia in 1742 and floated down the
Ohio till captured by Frenchmen and taken to New Or-
leans. On his return he wrote down all he could remember
about his journey on the interior waterways. Of course it
wasn't much, Fry pointed out, only what was glimpsed
from their crude buffalo-skin boat. However, Salley did
report a great deal of open country on each side of the
Ohio River, that it was level, well-watered, and appeared
to be fertile.

How little information that was, Fry exclaimed. Salley's descriptions could be true of almost any big river.
How maddening not to know more! How long was the
interior of America to be a blank piece of paper? He
begged Walker to bring him back information for the
map and report. And for the Loyal Company, of course.

They stopped their discussion to consume an apple
toddy before the fire and laugh over the story of how
Peter Jefferson bought the land where he lived for a
bowl of arrack punch. Fry wished information of the
western regions could be as easily obtained. He had once
heard someone claim that the climate of the interior of
America was terribly cold because thick, huge trees covered the land and kept the sun's rays from reaching the
ground. It was a tale he could not believe, yet some did.
Who knew without firsthand knowledge the truth of
this?

Did Fry believe the tale about the pass through the
Great Mountains, Walker wondered? The cartographer
thought it existed because so many Indian traders had
mentioned it, though no one he talked to had ever seen it
for himself. But where it was— He sighed. It was one

more piece of geographical knowledge of which he was ignorant.

Walker gazed silently into the dying fire. A candle sputtered on the mantel and went out. Rain fell softly on the roof. He would have to hunt long and hard for that mountain gap, that still-hidden needle. Yet it would most certainly be worth the time and effort. Yawning, he arose and helped his friend snuff out the rest of the candles. Then the two parted for the night.

3

Across the Piedmont and
Over the Blue Ridge

Rain still fell the following morning as the explorers rode away from Viewmont, and for the next few days, as they headed south, the weather was what Walker called "unlikely." Stopping often to visit acquaintances or to seek information about trails and land to the west, they moved along by easy stages across the Piedmont.

The Virginia Piedmont is an upland plateau that begins at the heads of the tidal rivers, where there are rapids and falls. From this "fall line" it slopes gently upward toward the Blue Ridge, its western boundary. In Walker's time it was different in many ways from the Tidewater coastal plain.

There were not many large plantations on the Piedmont. It was mostly an area of small farms that the owners worked themselves, or with perhaps only a slave or two. Tobacco was raised, but it was not the king crop it was in the tidal regions. Farming in the Piedmont was far more diversified. Houses were not as grand as those to the east. They were usually simple dwellings of a story and a half, frame-constructed in the traditional English manner with an outer covering of weatherboards. There might have been here and there a log cabin in the new clearings, for the Swedish style of house was moving westward. In Tidewater, cabins were thought fit only for slaves to live in, or for use as storehouses. But in the back parts, the quickly constructed cabin of round logs chinked with mud, moss, and wood chips was beginning to be considered a home good enough for anyone to live in.

There was another difference between the two Virginian regions—the people of the Piedmont and their attitudes were slowly altering. They were a little less British, a bit more American. It was as easy for them to cross the Blue Ridge to the land beyond as it was for them to reach the coast. More and more the Piedmonters were turning away from the mother country toward the west, hearing the beckoning call of the empty land.

The cold, wet ride across the Piedmont did not keep Walker from observing and commenting on this changing countryside. He was amazed at how fast it was being cleared of trees, at how many new milldams had been built since his last visit. He noticed new wagon roads, some still so new that they had not been entirely cleared of brush and others cleared but untraveled since they showed no traces of wheel ruts.

Even the language was changing. The fish Walker knew by the old English names of tench, perch, and mullet, the Piedmont folks now called carp, rocks, and fatbacks. Salt springs were licks; meadowlands along rivers had been called savannas for some time; river rapids were ripples generally, but he had heard a ripple called a riffle recently. The English cove, meaning a small bay or inlet, had left the ocean and gone into the Virginia mountains, where it signified a shut-in valley. If the British

words were misfits here in America, Walker saw no reason
not to adapt them to new uses.

The riders and the dog pack left the Piedmont on the
eighth day of their journey, crossing the Blue Ridge at a
gap so low and easily ascended that all remarked it was
difficult to tell they had crossed a height at all. Now
they were in the valley of Virginia—that trough which
was a part of the Great Valley of the Appalachians and
which extended from the New York region southward
to the Alabama foothills. The Indian trading and war
path traversed this thousand-mile valley, and white traders and explorers had long made use of it.

In these days pioneer settlers on foot and in wagons
were using it to leave Pennsylvania for North Carolina,
where land was cheap and easily procured. It was no
longer called the Indian path but was known in Pennsylvania as the Old Carolina Road; in North Carolina it was
the Great Philadelphia Wagon Road; and Fry and Jefferson on their map of Virginia were to label it grandly
"The Great Road from the Yadkin River thro' Virginia to Philadelphia distant 435 miles." A steady migration passed along this road, and a year or two after Dr.
Walker's group traveled a short bit of it, the Boone
family with teen-age Daniel was to use it to reach the
western wilderness of North Carolina.

The explorers guided their horses along the wagon
road toward the Great Lick. At this salt spring, buffalo
and elk had once thronged in great numbers. Now farms
bordered the marshy land. Walker, as they rode by, commented on how wasteful it had been for hunters to kill off
all the buffalo for mere diversion when today's inhabitants could have used them for meat.

Tomlinson remarked that he had heard that buffalo meat was coarse and stringy and hardly equal to beef in taste. Walker accused him jokingly of being a beef-and-biscuit Englishman, set in his ways and frightened of the novelties of experience. Before this journey was over, he'd have Tomlinson eating buffalo hump and rattlesnake steak and enjoying it. Tomlinson grimaced but agreed to try whatever Walker cooked.

The wagon road curved east beyond the Great Lick to cross the Staunton River and go through the Blue Ridge to Carolina. Turning from the double-rutted roadway, the explorers took a single track path winding through the trees to head south along the Great Valley.

Since leaving home, Walker had been purchasing salt, bacon, and various foods wherever he could find them. The six of them were keen shots, and Walker expected their guns to supply them daily with fresh meat. However, since they were going into unknown lands, where game might not exist or was scarce, he was taking no chances. He carried enough provisions on the packhorses for their survival through desperate times.

Especially had Walker tried to buy maize or Indian corn along their route. This grain always astounded visiting Europeans, since it was neither sown nor reaped as were their grains. The variety of its uses were proving so astounding to Virginians that American corn was taking the place of English wheat in the Piedmont and beyond in the Great Valley.

It had been found that wheat could not be grown in newly cleared ground. A field had to be entirely free of undergrowth, or else the weeds could choke out the slow-growing wheat. Furthermore, the soil had to be loose so the scattered seeds could be covered with a harrow. Who had time and patience to baby such a grain? Settled Europeans, it seemed, or Tidewater grandees with their large work force of slaves, but certainly not back-country Virginians opening up a new continent.

Corn now—what a grain! It could be planted in new ground among still standing, girdled, dead trees, or in most any kind of soil, and still manage to thrive. No need to worry about weeds, for corn grew fast enough to rise and stay above them. In addition to all that, it was tasty eating, too. Let the gentlemen planters of the Tidewater have wheaten bread on their tables; cornpone was good enough along the western border, where everyone raised corn and where its advantages for man and beast were just being discovered. Many new words were soon to be added to the American language as corn spread westward with pioneers and more and more uses were found for the grain, shucks, and stalks.

Walker already knew it was the ideal food for wilderness travel. It kept well, whether ground or carried as whole grains, and it was versatile enough to serve as a vegetable or a bread, to thicken meat stew, or to furnish an entire meal in the form of mush.

So one cold day Walker stopped at a settler's cabin to try to purchase corn. He was in luck, for he had a choice of small hominy (not yet called grits) or meal, which had been pounded and sifted. He took both. As he was paying, he asked who was the next inhabitant farther down the valley. He was informed that Samuel Stalnaker had just moved to one of the headsprings of the Holston River and was the last settler before the wilderness began.

This was great news to Walker. He had met Stalnaker two years before in that very same region as the German was heading for the Cherokee Indian towns to trade. He looked forward to seeing him again. Perhaps Stalnaker knew the location of the pass through the western mountains. Or better yet, perhaps he would guide them to it.

Walker hurried his group southward along the path. The prospect for a successful breach of the mountains now seemed good.

4

The Most Isolated
Western Virginia Settlement—
One Lonely Log Cabin

It was the middle of the afternoon of March 23 when the explorers left the Indian path to camp on the banks of the Holston River. They had been traveling slowly for seventeen days from farm to cabin to forest clearing. Walker had known the names of all the streams they crossed, of the mountains and ridges around them, and of most of the settlers. Although the dwellings had often been far apart and separated by miles and miles of woods, still the land was occupied, named, and known. Now they were on the edge of the unknown. The doctor knew the name of this stream—but the ones beyond were nameless, the country empty. The way ahead led into mist and nothingness.

They unsaddled, and Chew led the horses to the river. Then he hobbled them near the canebrake, where they could eat the leaves. The others, meanwhile, were setting up their tent. These men were not as hardy and expert as later wilderness travelers, who seldom hindered themselves with such an unnecessary luxury as a tent, but built with their axes a half-face shelter when needed, or more generally slept in the open. With the tent erected, Lawless went to get wood for a fire, while Hughes took off hunting with most of the dogs.

Doctor Walker removed his greatcoat. It was lined and very warm, fine to wear riding through the cold, but much too heavy and cumbersome for walking in the woods. He and Powell were going to try to find Stalnaker. He slipped into a waistcoat with sleeves and pulled a coat on over that. Then he retied the thongs of his Indian shoes, or "moccosons" as he called them.

All of Walker's men wore moccasins and must have been accustomed to them before this journey. Fashioned from one piece of leather, the moccasin sole was thin, so the feet inside them had to be tough. William Byrd II, who had gone exploring into the Virginia woods two decades earlier, had worn heavy thick-soled English boots to protect his feet. But these had proven difficult to walk in and, when torn by the rough ground and briers, had been impossible to repair without cobbler's tools. Moccasins were easily mended, quickly made. That Walker's group wore Indian shoes showed that British colonists were learning from the red men how to live with greater ease in the forested wilderness. Later, moccasins would become standard footwear for all frontiersmen.

However, the clothes of these men followed no set pattern. They were dressed in an assortment of old patched garments, the clothes they would have worn to work on their farms—various shirts and jackets and soft-brimmed hats. Walker and Hughes had on ankle-length trousers, the others tanned skin breeches that came only to their knees. All wore woolen stockings. They were dressed for ease and comfort.

Powell picked up his musket and cartridge box, and he and Walker set off to look for Stalnaker's clearing. The old scarred dog trotted along at Walker's side.

Cloud puffs of strange shapes scudded across the sky,

making the woods now dark, now bright. But even when
the sun shone, it was still bitter cold. The men walked
briskly for a while. Then the doctor stopped to inspect
fungus on a dead tree, again to pick red partridge berries
to munch, once more to wait while the dog followed an
animal scent off to a hollow tree. Walker's head turned
constantly as he strode along, and he missed little of interest about them. He pointed out a blooming sarvisberry
huddled ghostlike among the lifeless-looking black trees.
The dog discovered an old pair of elk antlers, and
Walker squatted to look at the little teeth marks of ro-
dents that had chewed them for salt.

They continued on their way, and Powell asked
Walker if he had met the man for whom the river was
named. The doctor nodded. He had met Stephen Holston two years ago when he came this way with some
friends. At that time Holston was hollowing out a poplar
log to make a dugout. He intended to float down *his*
river to see the sights. Walker wondered where he might
be by now.

Holston had lived at the headspring of the Middle
Fork of the river for two years. At that time the stream
was called Indian River because it flowed through Indian
country to the south. But soon after Holston's arrival,
surveyors were calling it Holston Creek. Later when three
prongs to the same stream were found, Holston's name
was applied to all three, and the stream's status was pro-
moted from creek to that of river. So now there was a
North Fork of the Holston River, a Middle Fork, and a
South Fork.

Walker and Powell talked about naming rivers and
other landmarks. Sometimes a first settler gave his own

name to a stream or mountain, but it was never called
that by others. Sometimes a stream was named by late ar-
rivals for the first settler on its banks, and the name
stuck, as in Holston's case. Walker felt sure the name
would continue in use, since he had seen it on the rough
draft of Fry and Jefferson's map. Also surveyors had
been using it in locating plots of land hereabout. Any
name involved with land titles stood an excellent chance
to survive.

Powell said he would be proud to have a river or
mountain named for him. Walker laughed and pointed
out that since they were heading into a nameless land,
the opportunities were great. It was an explorer's privi-
lege to name everything. He believed it was better to con-
nect a man's name with a stream than with a mountain.
Waterways were more important and useful and deserved
an explorer's name or that of a settler. Did Powell know
that Indians often called each section of a stream by a
different name? The red men did not see a river as a
thing in itself, one continuous flow of water from source
to mouth.

They walked on in silence until they reached a deadening, where all the trees had been girdled in the Indian
fashion. A strip of bark was cut away around the entire
trunk. The life-giving sap could not then flow past the
gap in the bark, and so the tree died. Walker reckoned
this would be Stalnaker's cornfield. Under the leafless
trees corn would grow, and it was the quickest and easiest way to make a first crop of the grain. Later the trees
could be cut down and burned, along with the stumps, for
a better field.

They passed through the deadening into the woods

and soon came to a small clearing. A few of the biggest trees had been cut down, but most were still standing. All the smaller ones had been felled and trimmed of branches and were now piled near the cabin's rectangular foundation—four partly hewed logs notched and fitted into each other. Once raised, the dwelling would sit snug among the huge trunks with just enough cleared space around it to provide daylight for the inhabitant.

They called and halloed about the clearing and fired the musket, but Stalnaker did not answer. Here was the furthest western Virginian settlement, Walker commented wryly, untended and only partly built. They would have to return the following day, find the trader, and see to it that the cabin was raised. Then it could go on Jefferson and Fry's map. And if they helped Stalnaker, perhaps he'd help them through the wilderness.

5

The Explorers Raise a House

The following morning Walker and his men packed their belongings and headed toward Stalnaker's. The sky was overcast, the day gray and cold. But in the deadening the dinginess was relieved for a moment by two woodpeckers. Their red, black, and white plummage flashed brightly as they swooped from tree to tree.

They rode on. Through the trees they saw a man lift a deer and hang it head downward from a limb. It was Samuel Stalnaker, and Walker called to him. The trader answered and began to skin the deer. By the time they threaded their way between the stumps and downed timber and crossed the clearing, Stalnaker had finished. He invited them to help themselves to a collop or two of deer meat. The dogs didn't wait for an invitation but fell on the entrails flung to one side with yipes of pleasure.

Walker dismounted and introduced his companions. One of the explorers led the horses off; the rest set up their tent. The doctor warmed his hands at the fire as Stalnaker roasted strips of meat. They discussed the news of the colony and various mutual acquaintances. Finally Walker got around to the Loyal Company and their expedition. He offered to pay Stalnaker to pilot them westward.

Stalnaker began to eat. Between swallows he explained that he had never been west of the Great Mountains and would certainly like to go with Walker, but he couldn't at the moment. He had promised to bring supplies to Old Hop, headman of the Cherokee town of Chota. Old Hop was trying to consolidate the many scattered Cherokee towns into a united nation with himself as the emperor. He desperately needed supplies. Stalnaker wanted to keep in good standing with Old Hop, for the trader believed the Cherokee chief would succeed in his efforts. An emperor would be a powerful friend for any white trader to have. So Stalnaker was going to keep his promise to Old Hop and take him supplies.

Walker was disappointed but not discouraged. If the path and the mountain pass existed, the explorers would find it. Before they moved on, however, they wanted to help with the house.

Stalnaker welcomed their help, and they divided up the tasks. The three best axmen were to work with Stalnaker, notching the logs. Walker selected Hughes, Tomlinson, and Lawless. The other two would fetch the logs from the pile, while he would do the chinking.

So the men set to work to raise a "round log" cabin, the quickest and easiest type to build. Hewn logs made a much snugger cabin, since the logs could be fitted close together. But hewing took extra work, and Stalnaker had not had the time to spend on this. Besides, he pointed out, he might move on again any time, and any extra work would be wasted.

The notchers stood at the corners of the cabin and

with axes chopped a nick top and bottom at each end of
the log. Thus the notch of a lower log fitted into the bottom notch of an upper log. Properly notched, cabin walls
held without the use of either nails or wooden pegs.

Slowly the walls began to rise. Walker brought a piggin of clay from the creek. Stuffing twigs and moss into
the cracks between the logs, he then plastered over these
with the clay to make the cabin weatherproof. So the
seven worked steadily through the morning, and they
didn't stop for the noonday meal till the walls were
raised. The afternoon was spent chopping a narrow
doorway through one side of the log wall, while a wider
opening was made at one end for a fireplace. Rafters went
up, and gabled ends were fitted to the ridgepole. They
finished with the roof ribs, which would hold the shingles.

Stalnaker had a white oak log he was seasoning. On
his return from the Cherokee country, he would rive his
shingles from it. A roof and a chimney, and he would be
ready to move inside. Perhaps next year, if he decided to
stay there, he would put in a puncheon floor. Meanwhile,
a dirt one would do.

In his journal Walker recorded that they helped Stalnaker "raise his house." This could only mean they built
a log cabin. To erect an English-type frame house required seasoned wood cut into beams, joists, and planks;
also many expensive, hard-to-get nails were required, as
well as a variety of different tools. Border folks could
not afford such an elegant house or one that required so
much time and effort. It was more important that fields
should be cleared and the crops harvested. So the easily
built, snug log cabin was a godsend to them.

Swedes had built the first log cabins in America in their

settlements around Delaware Bay in the early 1600's.
Coming from a region in Europe where trees were plentiful, they were accustomed to living in log dwellings. Germans, coming later into the rich farming areas of Pennsylvania, built log cabins of the type they were used to
building in forested Germany. Englishmen erected only
frame houses or those of brick as they had formerly done
across the sea. Usually immigrants to a new country built
houses similar to those of their homeland. In America
the Scotch-Irish were among the few who failed to follow
the rule.

Philadelphia was the principal port of entry for the
Scotch-Irish fleeing their "troubles" of 1715 and 1745.
But land near the city was already settled, and those plots
that remained uncleared were much too expensive for
these newcomers. So they headed for the frontier. Passing
through settlements of Germans and Swedes, they saw
their first log cabins and were quick to realize the advantages of such houses in the forests of America. They
had left lands where frame houses were a luxury, where
castles were grandiose and few, and where huts and hov-
els of sod and stone were common. The Scotch-Irish
took the log cabin as their very own type of dwelling and
were helping to spread its use down the Great Valley of
Virginia and into the back parts of North Carolina.

It is interesting that Walker and his Piedmont Englishmen already were experienced in the construction of
these log homes. However, the term "log cabin" had not
come into general use yet. Walker mentions "Indian cabins" in his journal, but a cabin to him and other eighteenth century Britishers meant a temporary shelter, a

hut or a booth. A "cabin" might also refer to a bunk or a room on a ship.

The phrase "log cabin" was headed westward with the pioneers and soon would lose its old meanings and take on a new one—that of a typical frontier dwelling of horizontal logs, either round or square hewn. "Cabin raisings," "raising bee," "raising frolic," and many other new expressions would come into existence as pioneers gathered together to help each other erect their frontier homes.

Thanks to Walker, Stalnaker's log cabin would appear on the map of Lewis Evan, a Pennsylvania surveyor and geographer, as "the furthest settlement in Virginia in 1755" and on many another map after that, though on account of engraving difficulties not on the Fry and Jefferson map of 1751.

6

Spring Is a Mad Chase
Across a Meadow

There was a flash of lightning before daybreak, followed by a terrifying crash. The ground shook as the thunder rolled off into the distance. The dogs yelped. One of the horses whinnied. Walker leaped from bed and slipped into his moccasins. Without tying the long laces, he flopped out of the tent.

A jagged streak of fire bolted across the sky and split into many smaller blazing tangles. Walker glanced toward the horses. All were still tied, but they were snorting and moving about in alarm. Now thunder sounded, far away this time, no more than low growls. The storm was passing over. He threw pine branches and wood on the fire. Rain splattered into the flames with soft hisses. It would be another cold, wet day in the saddle. He called to the men to hurry them along.

The day before had been fair, a fine day for traveling. But it was a Sabbath, and Walker did not believe in performing business on the Lord's day. The Loyal Company's exploration had to wait. They stayed right there at Stalnaker's. However, the trader had no compunction about carrying on his business. After a farewell and a final thanks for their help, Stalnaker left early Sunday morning to pick up the supplies for the Indians.

The men were up now, packing their gear, calming the horses. Walker set strips of deer meat on sticks around the fire. What was left of the deer, he then fed to the dogs. By the time the roasted meat was downed, the tent and equipment tied on the packhorses, all were thoroughly wet. But there was nothing to be done but climb on their mounts and ride on. Walker noted in his journal that it was March 26 when they left "the inhabitants"— Stalnaker's unfinished cabin, standing small and desolate in the rainy clearing.

The explorers followed the war and trading path southwestward through driving rain all that day and through snow part of the next. No amount of clothing kept out the chill nor shed the rain. Stiff and numb and bedraggled, they plodded on.

But worse than their bodily discomfort was the gloom that settled over the group as they pushed deeper into the wilderness. Huge trees pressed in close around them —poplar trees with trunks larger than Stalnaker's cabin, mottled beeches, warty oaks, and black walnuts, wrinkled with eroded-looking ridges along the boles. No one spoke as single file they rode through the somber woods.

At Stalnaker's, with enough of the big trees down for daylight to flood the clearing, the search for the western pass had seemed a mere trifle. But here among thick trunks, with the tops of the tallest trees lost in the cloudy mist overhead, man was puny indeed, and their expedition seemed hopeless and already doomed.

Walker was cheerful by nature, and if he worried much

about the success of their venture, he must surely have
kept his blackest thoughts to himself. Each afternoon he
ordered an early halt. Large fires were made at once.
When the ground thawed, the hot embers were brushed
away and the tent erected there. Thus, they slept dry each
night—a great help toward keeping his followers in
good spirits.

The doctor read aloud to them as they lay in their
beds. One night he lit a candle and, opening the Bible, began to read of the Israelites and their troubles. Wind
blew outside, steady enough to keep the canvas tent sides
shaking and swaying, though no drafts reached them.
Suddenly the dogs began to bark and stir restlessly about
the fire outside.

Walker paused, listening. What was upsetting the animals? Something, that was certain. He had best check.
In his greatcoat and shoes, he left the tent. His old
scarred hound stood at the outer rim of light, staring
into the woods, sniffing and growling. Lighting a bundle
of dry canes for a torch, Walker checked the horses,
then walked around the camp. He found nothing suspicious. Still the dogs were uneasy. Perhaps it was a cata-
mount attracted by the fire, or a wolf. Whatever it was,
there was no need to worry with the dogs on guard.

He returned to the tent to find the men in a heated
discussion about Indians. Powell maintained that Indians
were descendants of the Ten Lost Tribes of Israel and
had many customs similar to those of the Jews. Hughes
wanted to know how they had reached America, since it
was well known that the largest boat the red men could
construct was a dugout. Chew said if they had wandered

as far as eastern Asia, they could cross the isthmus that connected Tartary to the continent of North America.

Walker said he understood Asia and America were not joined, yet lay so close together that a dugout might well make the ocean voyage from one continent to the other. He added that he had heard from traders that many different Indian nations claimed their ancestors came from the far west. Indians might well have arrived in America from Asia if such was the case.

Tomlinson remembered hearing a parson tell that the Indians were descendants of Noah's eldest son Shem, that from Shem came Eber, whose younger son was Joktan, and from him sprang all the peoples of Asia. Lawless knew a preacher who despised the Indians because they worshiped the Devil as their idol and were therefor Satan's children, and where did that leave them in this discussion?

Ignorant about the Indians' origins and sleepy, Walker yawned. He blew out the candle, and they settled down for the night. The dogs had quieted, but the wind hadn't. They went to sleep to its sough.

They had not gone far the following morning when Tomlinson pointed to tracks in the snow along a creek. Indian footprints. Walker grinned. While they had been discussing the Ten Lost Tribes of Israel last night, Israelites had passed near them, though these didn't seem to be lost at all from the looks of their tracks heading north at a fast trot. He was sure it was the Indians who had aroused the dogs. Still, there had been no cause for alarm. Dogs might not care for intruding Indians, but no tribe had been at war with Virginians in decades and decades. The colony of Virginia was the red man's friend.

As the days passed, the woods became less gloomy, the trees thinned, the bushes didn't crowd the path so closely. More and more savannas appeared as they made their way along the banks of the Holston River. Overnight the weather turned warm, the breeze fresh and sweet. They had ridden into spring. Redbud bloomed throughout the woods, and in sheltered spots there were yellow violets and the swaying whiteness of blooming anemones. Alders tasseled almost before their eyes, and willows rushed forth before other trees to line the streams with a wispy show of bright green. One day a huge flock of geese flew overhead, filling the sky with great straggling, loud-honking V's. As they splashed through creek after creek, the explorers surprised into flight all kinds of waterfowl, many already paired and nesting.

It was spring. There was no doubt about it to the travelers. They were much cheered and rode along laughing and talking, the cold and damp forgotten. Now their wilderness ride became an adventure, a gay lark of fellowship and sightseeing. Each day brought novelty, a change in landscape, and they went forward eagerly, their appetites for strange sights keen, their hopes for adventures whetted.

One afternoon they stopped at the edge of a meadow spongy with moss and bluets and thick grass roots. They set up their tent beside a dogwood thicket from which flowed a mint-lined spring. Off through the trees could be seen the Holston, its whorled surface a gleam of flashing sunlight. A dove called from nearby. Walker took a hook and a line from his saddlebag. Tired of a diet of meat, he hoped to catch a string of fish for supper.

Chew wandered out on the meadow with some of the dogs. A moment afterwards he gave a wild yell. The dogs began to bark furiously. Walker rushed out of camp, the others right behind him. Through the knee-high grass came two buffalo calves, Chew whooping and hollering at their heels. The dogs snapped and leaped about the animals, driving them on. Walker and the others joined the chase.

The calves zigzagged back and forth across the grassland, sometimes side by side, again swerving away from each other as the men closed in around them. It was a wild melee. Dogs got in the way, tripping the men and sending them sliding through the grass. One of the buffalo was caught but butted the doctor in the stomach and escaped, to race away with Hughes holding onto its tail. Tomlinson grabbed for a calf, missed, and got trampled on by the animal.

At last both calves were caught, thrown to the ground, and their feet tied. The chase was over, but the dogs were unwilling to stop. They leaped and yelped about the buffalo, trying to make them rise and run again. The men threw themselves to the ground, tired, panting, but laughing uproariously at their spring madness, at their foolish chase. Still they were quite delighted to have caught their supper using only their feet and fists. Not a shot had been fired, yet the warm night would be filled with the smell of roasting buffalo, and they would feast like gluttons.

7

A Chain of Troubles

Three days later Walker decided it was time for them to leave the Indian path that they had followed since the Great Lick in the Virginia Valley. Why he chose this time and place he never revealed in his writings. Perhaps something Stalnaker had told him influenced his judgment. There is no way to know just what information Walker secured from the trader, but it was likely enough to encourage the doctor with his westward probing.

Still, Thomas Walker had a chancy nature. Risks had never dampened his enthusiasm for and curiosity about the new, the different. Already he had been a storekeeper, a farmer, a physician, a druggist, and now an explorer. He was to try many difficult assignments for Virginia and learn other professions before his death. After their leisurely Sabbath of fishing and name-carving on tree trunks, Monday, April 2, may simply have seemed a propitious date on which to begin to explore the unknown west, to prove that they were hardy Colonial British, able to survive the challenges of the American wilderness. Above all Walker would be anxious to find the pass as soon as possible so they might have plenty of time to look beyond the mountains for settlement sites for the Loyal Company. Straight westward would be the quickest course.

Walker's decision to leave the easily traveled path marked the beginning of a chain of troubles that were to plague them for some time. They had no sooner left the meadows of the Holston and ridden in among small scattered hills than one of the horses choked on cane leaves. The men had to throw the animal to the ground and hold it while Walker poured great amounts of water down its throat. The wad of stiff leaves was washed down and the horse was all right, but it was unable to travel further that day.

They kept westward the following morning till a ridge blocked their way. Walker climbed on foot to the top but couldn't find a way to get the horses over such rocky cliffs. They would have to go around the ridge. He knew there were many mountain ranges north of them, so he lead the group in the opposite direction in the hope the mountains would be dispersed and less high. They followed a small stream down a narrow valley. But they made so little progress through the tangles of "laurel" and "ivy" that at last Walker gave up. Surely the ridge would be easier after all. Leading, pushing, coaxing the horses, they managed to get them over the rocks and safely down the other side. It had been a long, exhausting day. As they were making camp, Walker's horse choked on cane leaves. It took all of them, as before, to save it with drenchings of water.

Rain hindered them, then hail and snow. Walker's old dog was mangled by a bear so badly that it had to be carried in the doctor's arms. A raft they built to float their possessions across a wide river sank after the first trip. They forded the icy stream with their belongings on their shoulders.

Ridge after ridge they labored over; stream after

stream they crossed. They cut their way through canebrakes, through matted laurel slicks, and through cur-
tains of catbrier and poison ivy. Tired, saddle-sore,
scratched, and bruised from ten days of wilderness floundering, they still had not discovered the path or the
mountain gap by the afternoon of April 12, when they
camped beside a river.

Walker mentioned in his journal that this was the
clearest stream they had found. From the coarse, stiff
plants growing on the banks, he promptly named it Beargrass River. So far Walker had not named a stream or a
mountain for himself or his followers. He had bestowed
many names on creeks in his unimaginative way, such as
Holly, Ivy, and Laurel Creeks. The worst of the many
mountains they crossed he called simply Rocky Ridge.
A practical man, he preferred plain descriptive names.

The river they had attempted to raft across he guessed
might be the Clinch, so named for a hunter who had discovered its headwaters. Walker had been along the upper section of the Clinch years before and was later to
own various tracts of land there. He knew the Clinch was
the largest south-flowing river west of the Holston. It
was a guess, but a reasoned guess, and was correct,
though he had no way to know that he was right.

While Walker explored along Beargrass River and the
others hunted, Powell spent his time carving his name on
the trees along its bank. Perhaps he yearned to have this
beautiful stream named for him. If so, he would have
kept his wish to himself. The doctor did the naming
and kept the journal, and that was that. Into the bark of
beech after beech, he cut A. POWELL till darkness came,
and then he returned to camp. In later years hunters

found the name on so many trees, they began referring to it as Powell River, and so it remains today. The name Beargrass River disappeared, but ironically Ambrose Powell probably never knew how he immortalized himself that afternoon by his few hours' work with a knife.

The hunters returned with turkeys and a deer. Walker came back with specimens of yellow flint and pieces of coal and with a wallet filled with various roots, leaves, and barks. These herbal materials he had brought were stimulants. After what the men had recently been through, they all needed something to brace them, to inspirit them for the days ahead. As their doctor, he recommended that they all have some of the tea he planned to make of the medicants he had found in the woods.

He filled an iron pot with water and placed it over the hot wood ashes. As he dropped the items into the pot, he explained that while each was of a stimulating nature, some also possessed other useful properties. Wintergreen leaves were added for sweetness; the roots of ginger would soothe acid stomachs; sweet gum and sweet shrub bark had no extra qualities beyond being stimulants that he knew; but mint leaves imparted flavor; bloodroot would aid the digestion; and mullein leaves he had added purely for their help in cleansing the kidneys. However, he wished that he could find ginseng, but it was too early for the plant to show in the woods. Though ginseng was not a stimulant, of all plants it was supposed to possess the most powerful cure for any of man's ailments.

Hughes wanted to know why this was so, since in the woods ginseng was such an innocuous-looking plant. It was the plant's root and its connection with the Doctrine of Signatures, Walker replied, which he would explain as they waited for the turkeys to roast and the tea to boil.

The theory of the Doctrine of Signatures held that God had left a mark, a signature, on every plant to show the special use for which He had created it. Heart-shaped leaves cured cardiac trouble. Hepatica with its spotted liver-like leaves aided liver ailments. Ginseng roots were shaped like a man. Therefore, according to the theory, ginseng must surely be able to cure whatever troubles a man might have.

No one had yet studied American plants in such detail as to completely prove or disprove the Doctrine of Signatures, Walker went on. He believed ginseng was as useless as it was harmless. Many plants possessed curative qualities that had nothing to do with their shape or color. Indians held that an orchid, called rattlesnake plantain, eased snake bites because its leaves were as marked as a serpent's skin. He himself used the plant to treat snake bites, not because of the Doctrine of Signatures, but because the plant seemed to help.

The tea was now ready, and the doctor wanted them to know it was purely an herbal tea and had nothing to do with the signature doctrine. As they drank and ate, the talk shifted away from herbs and simples to that of strange cures. Tomlinson had heard of a woman who could stop bleeding by repeating a certain verse of the Bible. Hughes thought the power could only come from a seventh son of a seventh son. Chew knew a granny-woman who cured croup merely by blowing in the patient's mouth. Powell wondered if a birthmark could be removed, as he had been told, by rubbing it with the hand of a corpse. Walker snorted. Such cures were silly nonsense.

Neither he nor other trained physicians used such methods.

The men pronounced the doctor's tea excellent. Some even took a second cup. Walker tried to get his wounded dog to drink a little, but it refused, preferring raw meat instead. The doctor finished off the pot himself.

The following morning they were packed and ready to ride long before sunrise. The men told Walker it was due to his herbal tea, which had so stimulated them that they were unable to sleep. The doctor grinned at their teasing. It was his impatience that had aroused the men earlier than usual. He wanted to be off and find that pass.

Walker mounted his horse, and Chew handed up the wounded dog. It licked the doctor's hand as he settled it across his lap. He was pleased at its recovery, since it had been so terribly mauled and ripped by the bear. With any other dog, he might have given up and put it out of its misery. Not his favorite. A few more days under his treatment and the dog should be walking again.

He glanced around their campsite to make sure nothing had been overlooked. Yesterday an iron spider and a bag of lead shot had been forgotten. It was ridiculous to add to their troubles by carelessly leaving behind needed items.

Another campfire of charred sticks and gray ashes; another night spent in the wilderness and still nothing to show for their hardships and strivings. Perhaps today something more encouraging than rocky ridges and laurel thickets would turn up. He was hopeful. He pulled on the reins and moved off, the other explorers falling in behind him.

8

The Needle and
Through the Eye to Beyond

They forded the Beargrass River at a shallow spot and on the opposite bank headed west. It soon became rocky, and the hardwoods gave way to huge cedar trees. Later they left the rough terrain and passed onto an open stretch of red-gold grasses and tangled spreads of blooming strawberry runners. Meadowlarks called, and once a covey of quail exploded from under Walker's horse, causing it to shy and almost unseat him and the dog. He quieted the horse, and they moved on.

In the distance a dark hump appeared. The closer they came, the higher it rose, until, formidable and menacing, it filled the whole horizon. Another mountain to struggle over! The men groaned. Walker said nothing, only patted the dog and rode determinedly on toward it.

Then they chanced upon what Walker referred to as a "plain Indian road." He halted. They had headed west all morning. This path ran north and south. Should he follow it? He had hoped to reach the mountain ahead and be over it before sundown. Still this might be the path of which he had heard so many rumors.

Although the doctor didn't know it, he had found the

Warrior's Path. Coming from the Iroquois villages in the colony of New York, it ended in the Carolinas, where the Catawba Indians lived. When the Indians said "Warrior's Path," the term had a milder meaning than when employed by the whites, who believed such a route was strictly a warpath. All able-bodied Indians were designated "warriors" by courtesy, and any path they used for whatever purpose was therefore, in fact, a warrior's path. Most warrior's paths were routes chosen as the straightest, easiest, and quickest ways between distant points.

Walker decided it could do no harm to try the trail northward for a short distance. It would be easier traveling for the horses. If it veered in the wrong direction, they could always leave it. Single file, they moved off along the beaten track.

It was hot, more like summer than April. Lawless rode behind the doctor, slouched in his saddle, dozing. Powell and Chew chatted about Williamsburg and the dances they had attended there. Hughes listlessly cleaned his carbine. Tomlinson walked at the rear, stretching his legs and leading his horse and the pack animals.

Only Walker was alert, speculating on this savanna. It was certainly the largest, best piece of land they had seen. It would make a fine settlement site. Some could farm and others mine coal. Surely that piece he had found yesterday indicated coal seams somewhere nearby. The Beargrass River was deep enough in freshet to boat the coal off for sale. There were plenty of springs here and trees for houses at the meadow's edge. Way off he saw three elk moving slowly and stately through the grass. Beyond them there appeared to be a small herd of buffalo, so there was game here also. What an excellent site for the Loyal Company!

One of the dogs scared up a rabbit near the trail and went scooting after it with great yelps. Several other dogs joined the chase. The rest trotted placidly on with the men and horses. The trail circled a miry place where Mary's gold and wild iris flowered beside dark pools. From dried cattail stalks, red-wing blackbirds watched the group pass. It was peaceful, pleasant—a wonderful day to be riding leisurely far beyond the settlements. If only they could find the pass, their enjoyment would be complete.

By midmorning Walker noticed a break in the mountain wall off to his left. It was just a slight nick, a dip in the mountaintop, yet he kept his eyes on it hopefully. If it proved promising, he would leave the Indian road and head straight for it.

They plodded on. The sun rose higher. Heat waves shimmered over the grass tops. High up, a lone buzzard winged in circles, to sail off at last over the mountain. Gradually the break widened and grew deeper. The men quieted and bunched up close behind their leader. Their slow progress was maddening. If Walker had not been carrying the wounded dog, he would have galloped forward with all haste.

Now the path turned sharply and headed directly for the break, so that they had a full view of a great mountain gap. Walker had no doubts whatsoever. They had discovered the needle in the haystack—the fabled pass existed! Here was an easy way through the mountains to those western lands that were blank spaces on Fry's map.

Walker was relieved; the men were happy and talkative. If they found nothing else, this gap made their journey worthwhile. The date of that day, noted in the journal, was April 13, 1750.

When at last they reached the bottom of the slope with cliffs towering overhead, white and sparkling in the noon sunlight, were they impressed by this magnificent mountain pass? Walker didn't say so in his record, merely stating that the north wall of the gap was steep and rocky and much higher than the south side. He named it Steep Ridge.

Eighteenth century Colonial Americans seldom appreciated the beauties of nature, or at any rate not in their writings, for they were much more interested in the practical value of a new place. Walker proved typical of the times. He had not only discovered an important and long-sought way through the mountains, but on its slope he had also found a cave from which came a stream of water "sufficient to turn a mill." A useful fact for later days. But more than that: from the cave came a constant current of cold air—a blowing cave! This might prove beneficial. Certainly it was a curiosity, and the doctor was intrigued, so intrigued that the pass was called Cave Gap.

The explorers followed the Warrior's Path up the slope to the saddle of the gap. Here they saw trees with Indian picture writing painted on them. Others had crosses carved on the bark; a few trees were blazed. They hurried on to the western slope and here paused long enough for Walker to cut his name into the side of a huge beech.

The group pushed on, and if they expected a different kind of country from that east of the gap, they didn't find it. More creeks with thick canebrakes along the banks. More rocky ground so that on Easter Sunday they had to move their camp to where the horses had better forage— clover and hop vines. There was more rain also, and on April 17 they arrived, miserable and dripping, on the banks of a large westward-flowing stream. The French knew it in its lower reaches as Rivière des Chauouanons —the River of the Shawnee.

Walker didn't know this. He gave it a new label. He named it for the Duke of Cumberland, William Augustus. The Duke had led the British Army against Bonnie Prince Charlie and burned and hanged his way across the Scottish Highlands to victory over the clansmen. His brutality earned him the nickname of "Billy the Butcher." Once again, Walker felt no obligation to say why he chose such a name. Whatever the reason, the name stuck to the river, later spread to the pass, which became known as Cumberland Gap, and in time came to be used for the mountain range Walker had called Steep Ridge.

Here, at the Cumberland River, the Warrior's Path crossed to continue northward. Walker guessed it must lead to the Ohio River country and was therefore not for them. John Peter Salley, Fry's friend, had visited those regions and described them in his journal. The doctor had not forgotten his contract with the Loyal Company, which stated he was to go westward. At the ford he turned and led his company under the dripping trees downstream.

A few days later, because one of the horses had gone lame, Walker split his group. Lots were drawn to see who would stay and build a cabin and plant corn and peach stones and who would ride on. Powell and Chew were the fortunate ones to go westerly with the doctor. But after a few days of constant fighting through the thick undergrowth, the idea of raising a cabin had an easy appeal that exploration lacked. Even Walker was discouraged at their slow progress. They had come out of the mountains into foothills, but these foothills seemed to stretch on endlessly. The horses were jaded, the laurel thickets getting worse. It was useless to continue unless better land lay ahead.

Walker found a hilltop with a tree higher than those around it. He would decide here and now whether to go on or turn back. Powell and Chew, both younger, urged him to let them climb the tree. The doctor had no intention of doing that. This was his expedition. He had chosen his companions, he had named what needed to be named, he had led them to the pass, and he had ministered to their needs. He hoped in time to get them safely home. But now he would see for himself what was beyond, what was out there—westerly.

So, Doctor Thomas Walker, from the Piedmont in Colonial Virginia, accustomed, in knee breeches, lace shirt, and buckled shoes, to associate with wealthy planters and now very much at ease in loose dirty pants and jacket and Indian shoes, shinnied up the tree to the very top. What did he discover? He later recorded in his journal that "as far as my sight could reach" the land was the same as it had been for the past two days. It was disappointing. He would have to turn back. There was not enough time for him to explore farther.

Here then was the end. High in a tree, swaying in the breeze, staring hopefully westward, Walker's expedition reached as far into the interior as it could go. Though he was to spend over two more months getting home through the rough lands of eastern Kentucky and West Virginia, the important part of Walker's journey was over. While he never saw the blue-grass regions of Kentucky, still he had discovered the gap and a piece of the Warrior's Path that would help others reach those rich lands later.

9

A Bold Spirit Began
the Wilderness Road

Walker and his men continued to be pestered by misfortunes as they slowly made their way north, then eastward, toward the Virginia settlements. A horse and rider fell down a bank; both were injured and required the doctor's care. They lost more of their possessions. At various times rattlesnakes bit several of the horses, and Walker used a decoction of the roots of rattlesnake plantain for their relief when he could find the plant. When he couldn't, he used bear's oil as a helpful draft and applied it to the wound also. Once he resorted to a piece of fat meat to relieve the poisonous swelling.

They had trouble with wolves. An elk killed a dog. The horses finally were so spent that the men were forced to walk. Still the group struggled on, never quite lost, yet never entirely sure just where they were.

In time, each of Walker's followers had a stream named for him, though these don't occur on today's maps. They never even appeared on published copies of Fry and Jefferson's map. In the "Journal" attached to the map, Fry mentioned that he had received a great deal of information from Thomas Walker and that the doctor had built "a house" on the Cumberland River. Yet when

the map was printed, none of Walker's names were there
nor the location of the cabin either.

The horizontal width of Fry and Jefferson's map
greatly exceeded its vertical dimensions, and the London
engraver was unable to prepare wide enough plates to
encompass the whole map. Thus, the western portions
were chopped off to make a more uniform-size map.
There went the Virginian cartographers' handiwork, as
well as Walker's western place names.

However, the chopped-off portion of the map was not
long displaced. When Major George Washington's "Journal" of his Ohio journey was reprinted in 1754 in London, there was included with the text a map of the western parts of Colonial Virginia. This map was published
and engraved by the same man who had issued Fry and
Jefferson's text and map. No cartographer was mentioned for the map with Washington's "Journal," but the
names appearing on it could only have come from
Walker. And the eight- by twelve-foot cabin, which three
of Walker's men had erected, was recognized as "Walker's Settlement 1750"—quite splendid for such a small
building, inhabited by lizards, raccoons, and deer mice.

Since the same engraver was used for both maps, it is
obvious that the chopped-off portion of Fry and Jefferson's map was used with the Washington "Journal." This
was the first printed map containing such western data.
Walker filled in some blank spaces in the interior of
America for his friend, Joshua Fry. Even later maps
used Walker's names, and these cartographers acknowl-
edged the doctor's help. It must have been most gratify-
ing to Walker that his geographical discoveries were useful and furthered the claim of Virginia and of Britain
against those of France for the western lands.

By early July the explorers were safely back among Virginia frontier settlers. They had journeyed together almost five months, and now each was to go his separate way. Powell was to be surveyor of Culpepper County, Virginia. Chew became a captain in Washington's regiment and was killed in the 1758 expedition against Fort Duquesne. The Revolutionary War was to find Tomlinson fighting at Bryan's Station, Kentucky, in which state he lived till his death. A Henry Lawless was killed by Indians in West Virginia in 1757 and might have been the one who went with Walker. Hughes moved off into oblivion.

Walker was to keep the Loyal Company active for some time longer, but conflicting land claims brought too much trouble, and he gave up the leadership. However, the successors to the original members kept up litigation about the company well into the nineteenth century. But Walker had had through the years other interests besides land. He became a surveyor. He served as commissary-general to Washington's troops during the French and Indian War. He was a member of various Virginia governing bodies at various times, even after Virginia became a state, and he represented Virginia at Indian treaties.

In 1753 it was suggested that Virginia's sea-to-sea claim of land would be greatly strengthened if a water route across America to the Pacific was found before the French succeeded in their search. Joshua Fry recommended to the governor that the commander of the expedition be that "person of fortune and great activity"— Doctor Thomas Walker. Such hopeful, far-roaming plans never matured. A stop was put to them by the French and Indian War, which was to take up much of Virginia's energies and ambitions.

Now, in the summer of 1750, Walker's quest was over. He was back among Virginian acquaintances. One by one his companions left him as he rode eastward. He was forced to abandon his horse and borrow another to continue. At last only his old scarred dog remained of those that had set out a-journeying with him the previous March. Together these two travelers went on across the Great Valley, climbed the Blue Ridge, and arrived at Walker's farm July 13.

The fields of tobacco were flourishing. Corn was shoulder-high, the leaves green and bright in the sunlight, the young ears big and promising. Jar flies droned sleepily from the oaks. An oriole sang from the orchard in back of the house. Mrs. Walker and the children were having a noonday nap, a servant said. The doctor got stiffly from the saddle and squatted to hug the old dog fondly. Two weary travelers were home from the unknown and mighty glad to be back. He stood up and walked toward the house to rouse his family.

Thomas Walker lived to the age of 79. At his death his journal was still unpublished. However, through widespread acquaintances he furnished much information to many cartographers besides Fry and Jefferson. He had brought history to Cumberland Gap with the first written record of its existence. Inadvertently he had furnished it with a name. He had helped to advance America a bit closer to its destiny. He was a bold spirit, a man of action rather than ideas, but a fitting person to have begun the inventing of the Wilderness Road.

10

A Summing Up:
The Half–American

Gentleman William Byrd II, Tidewater planter, served as a commissioner for Virginia in that colony's first survey of its boundary line with North Carolina in 1728. He took Indians with him into the wilds to do his hunting and servants to cook and set up the tents. Many bags of cooked wheaten biscuits were carried, as well as other foodstuffs. After this expedition ended, Byrd commented: "The chief discouragement at present from penetrating far into the woods is the trouble of carrying a load of provisions. . . . But the common precautions against it (famine), are so burthensome, that people cannot tarry long out, and go far enough from home, to make any effectual discovery." Being a beef-and-biscuit British Colonial, he was in awe of the American wilderness, did not trust it, and felt rather helpless floundering around in it.

Walker, twenty-two years after Byrd, knew wheat biscuits were cumbersome to tote and would mold and be useless for wilderness fare, so he carried Indian corn for emergencies. But he also expected the woods to supply him with game, and in this he was not disappointed. The closing words of his journal were: "We killed on the journey 13 buffaloes, 8 elks, 53 bears, 20 deer, 4 wild geese, about 150 turkeys, besides small game. We might have killed three times as much meat if we wanted it." His faith in himself and his faith in the American wilderness had been a gamble that paid off. Such *faith* would later become a typical attribute of those pioneers headed west, a bedrock on which to build an expanding nation.

Walker's journal mentioned a canister that was lost. This indicated they were using either muskets or carbines, weapons not too accurate except at close range. Bullets of lead and powder, rolled in paper, were carried in a metal canister, upright inside in holes, ready for quick use. The long rifle and shot pouch and powder horn had not yet come into general use by wilderness travelers. And the time had not arrived when men went into the forests strictly to hunt, depending on their skill with the rifle to keep them in meat and to furnish them with skins for profitable trading. The long hunter was later, but not too far off.

Ralph Waldo Emerson writing in the nineteenth century about our past said: "Europe extends to the Alleghanies; America lies beyond." Walker and his followers of the Piedmont were closer to the west, to the future America, both in time and space, than aristocratic Byrd of the tidal region. And their accomplishments were considerably more American also. The journal showed that the six men knew how to raise a log cabin; how to construct an elm-bark canoe; how to smoke tough elkskin to fashion the best, longest-wearing Indian shoes; and how to use plants as simples. It was a remarkable list, but a great deal more know-how was needed to push beyond the Appalachians to take the western land.

Although the doctor and the other explorers had

shucked away some of their English skin, they were still only half American, not yet fully experienced in wilderness life, not yet woodsmen. On their expedition they had one mishap after another. They lost a great many of their possessions. Such carelessness was dangerous. The wilderness could be most beneficent to those who understood its potentials, but for the novice it usually proved harsh and unfriendly. Those who hoped to travel through it with ease would need to learn much more than Walker's people knew.

In 1750, when Walker ended his journey, that wonder of the woods, the long hunter, had not yet emerged. There were no Indian fighters, no forts along Virginia's peaceful frontier. Kentucky was unnamed, and still very little was known about it. The Wilderness Road had only begun to exist. The contest for interior America between England and France was steadily deepening. War was becoming inevitable, and when it came, it would mark an end and a beginning.

NEWSCAST OF 1763

An insight into the changed attitudes of Virginians
at the close of the French and Indian War
and the reasons behind these changes

WAR ENDS—HOPEFUL FUTURE AHEAD

The year 1763 opens with great news for the American
colonies. The French and Indian War, called by Europeans the Seven Years' War, ends with Great Britain
victorious. With the signing, February 10, of the Treaty
of Paris, France relinquishes her North American possessions to England. The colonies are relieved that the
French threat is gone from their western borders and a
peaceful life can be resumed.

Virginia is especially jubilant over the outcome. Now
nothing can stop the colony's inland thrust of settlements.
Land companies are back in business and hopeful of
riches. Since Walker's exploration in 1750 and the Ohio
Company's probe of the Ohio River country in 1750–51,
both companies have been idle, awaiting the outcome of
the war. Now their future appears most promising.

A NEW VIRGINIAN SHAPE

Virginians have returned to the daily tasks of plantation and farm, and the colony's business is back to its normal pace. Yet many feel that life is not the same today as it was before the French and Indian War. There is a difference now. The long conflict shaped a new creature—a new Virginian.

BRITISH HATE AMERICAN COUSINS

Fighting side by side with the red-coated British soldiers during the French and Indian War, the Virginians had been shocked and amazed to find that their cousins from across the sea thought them ignorant backwoods folks who knew nothing about warfare; cowards who wouldn't volunteer to help the British army and couldn't fight their own battles; simple farmers who didn't know how to govern themselves and so had to submit to a royal governor sent out from England.

Virginians knew that the truth was far different. During the war they had mustered their own troops, supplied them with food and weapons, and then planned, fought, and won battles all on their own initiative. It had not taken them long to learn that the British soldier was pretty useless in forest fighting. Braddock's defeat in 1755, when 1,500 British regulars were demolished by a few hundred Frenchmen and naked savages, taught the Virginians to put no trust in European methods and tactics.

They knew, as well, that for some time the Virginia Assembly had been slowly taking away the royal governor's powers, with the result that these "ignorant farmers" actually had more independence and participated more in government than did the English people themselves.

FARE-THEE-WELL, MOTHER ENGLAND

Today Virginians feel they can handle any situation with which they are confronted. If not, they won't turn to Britain for help. They will go to the other American colonies. Virginia has already met with other colonies to deal with common problems not touched on in the British Constitution. The war has taught the colonies to cooperate with each other in civil and military matters. Seldom has this happened before, since most of the Thirteen Colonies have not only been suspicious of each other but also fearful that one colony will be favored by England over the others.

So the French and Indian War has brought about a different attitude toward the mother country, as well as fostered a disrespect for the Britishers. The Englishmen who came to America during the war turned out to be foreigners who looked haughtily down their noses at Virginians, laughed at their customs, speech, and manner of living, and scorned everything American as backward and quaint. This is not forgotten or forgiven in Virginia. It is true of the other colonies as well. Some of the ties that bound England and her American settlements together have gone.

HORRORS ALONG THE WESTERN BORDER

Perhaps Virginians along the western border are more changed by the recent war than those in the Piedmont or

Tidewater regions, for most of the fighting and the suffering in the colony took place on that frontier. Such terror had not been known since the Indian wars of the 1600's, and the borderers were so unprepared for the war whoop and the scalping knife that they could do little more than flee in panic across the Blue Ridge.

Soon after the war began, Indians rushed through the Appalachian passes to quickly attack and burn lone cabins and clusters of farms along the whole frontier. Just as quickly they disappeared, leaving behind dead and mutilated men and women, young children with their skulls bashed in, and crippled, arrow-filled livestock. Pursuit of the war parties had been useless for those brave enough to stay and try it. Trails were unfamiliar and vague. And these frontiersmen didn't yet know how to fight the Indians in the woods. There was not a single fort or blockhouse to provide refuge, for it had been decades and decades since Indians were a danger in Virginia. It proved a nerve-shattering experience, and it is no wonder so many left the frontier.

INDIANS TEACH SETTLERS HATRED

Still many stayed to hold their farms, and they learned to build log forts and picket stockades. In time the borderers began to post lookouts along trails to watch for war parties and to warn the people. Then families rushed to the forts to live crowded together till danger was past. Though they hated every cramped moment behind the log walls, they survived.

As the war continued, the frontiersmen learned to ambush the savages and fight them Indian-style from tree to tree. It took courage at first to stand in amongst the trunks watching the shadows, waiting for a cruel, painted face, listening for a soft moccasin tread. But every skirmish won by these methods gave them confidence. Their fear of Indians lessened over the years, while their hatred increased.

A BREED APART

So the war has made keen fighters and woodsmen of border Virginians. It has shown them they need fear neither the wilderness nor the savages. With this self-assurance has come a boldness, a toughness that sets them apart not only from the British of today but also from eastern Virginians as well. These border people feel that they are a little more American than are eastern Virginians, who they believe are softened by ease and luxurious living. At the present time the frontiersmen see themselves as a breed apart, accustomed to fatigue, hardships, difficulties, and danger.

THE NEW BREED STRIKES

The withdrawal of the French leaves most of the Indians north of the Ohio River without a friend. Though they stand alone, they are determined not to let white American colonists take over their country. One Ottawa chief, Pontiac, organizes the many scattered tribes. The month of May this year finds him attacking the strongholds across the northwest that are occupied by British soldiers. By June his Indian war parties reach Virginia and begin their burning and killing along the frontier.

The borderers—the new breed—know what to do. A thousand men are organized into companies of about thirty individuals each. These pursue the raiders to kill

them and take back the stolen booty and the white cap-
tives. The companies push into the Ohio River country,
burn the Indian towns, destroy the fields, and take as
many savage scalps as they can. Virginia's border is safe.
With the arrival of fall, Pontiac surrenders, and the up-
rising is over.

There is fresh respect in Virginia for the borderers.
But there is an uneasiness, too. Are they not as violent
and savage as the Indians?

LONDON TREMBLES

Pontiac's War frightens the government in London. It
sees nothing but trouble from the Indians and the Americans in the future. It does not want any more costly wars.
A proclamation is issued that declares that interior
America belongs to the red men. There shall be no
trespassing or settlements on the land beyond the heads
of the rivers that flow into the Atlantic from the west
and the northwest. This means, roughly, that the Allegheny Mountains form the western boundary of the colonies. Great Britain wants the colonists to stay close to
the seacoast, within easy reach of the trade and com-
merce and influence of the kingdom.

ONLY A SCRAP OF PAPER

Copies of the proclamation reach America October 11.
Virginians are furious that Britain has awarded the savages all the good land in interior America. It belongs to
Virginia. What right has England to tell Virginia what
to do with her very own province? The colony can handle
its own affairs. Anti-British feeling increases.

The more thoughtful see the line drawn by the proclamation as only a means of pacifying the Indians for the moment. They think that in the future it will be lifted. Others point out it is only a scrap of paper that means nothing, for there are not enough British soldiers in America to patrol the line and keep intruders out.

And as October, 1763, ends, a group of Virginians are already beyond the proclamation line. They are heading west on a long hunt. Their leader is Elisha Wallen.

PART TWO

ELISHA WALLEN
Long Hunter—All American

A Flat Rock With
a Hole in It

The Clinch River twisted and growled over the rocks. Elisha Wallen sat quietly on his horse in the shadows, scanning the islands opposite him and then the shore beyond. An Indian path forded the river here and followed it downstream along the western bank. That morning, farther back on the path to the east, he had found Indian tracks heading this way, but he had been unable to trace them very far.

He slid to the ground, and with his rifle tucked under one arm, he studied the dirt bank leading down to the water. There were no footprints here at all, only deer tracks. Satisfied, he led the four horses down to drink.

Upstream the river was glassy smooth and still. Two parakeets came shooting low over the green water, heading straight toward him, their heads glowing like orange-red fireballs. They were close enough for him to see their bright button eyes when they suddenly swooped up over his head and were gone with a hoarse squawk and a flurry of green wings.

A horse whinnied in the woods behind him, and one of the animals, drinking, raised its head and answered. That would be the six other members of his hunting party. He was ahead of them because he was riding, while they were on foot. Each man had brought two horses packed with all the gear they might need for their long stay in the wilderness.

Wallen usually had only two horses himself on hunts, but this time he hoped to bring back four loads of skins. That would be about four hundred skins, enough to trade for a new rifle and all his other necessities for a while. Hunting was his livelihood. His wife had a truck patch back of their cabin on the Smith River in the Virginian Piedmont, but Wallen didn't believe in tilling the soil so long as there was game to shoot and skins to trade.

William Blevins came along the path with his animals. He was chewing vigorously. He stopped at the edge of the river and spit an arc of amber into it. Wallen grinned. His father-in-law was never without a chew of tobacco. In all likelihood one of his pack horses was carrying nothing but twists of tobacco, and how many deer could a hunter kill with tobacco?

Blevins's son, Jack, came up next with his long rifle across his shoulder. Close at his heels were Henry Skaggs and William Pittman. They crowded together on the riverbank.

Skaggs suggested that they cross unless the Clinch River was the location of the proclamation line. If it was, then they had better not go over, for they didn't want to break the King of England's law. There were hoots of laughter from the others.

Before the hunters left their homes in the Piedmont, they had heard about the line. A neighbor who had just returned from Williamsburg, the capital of Virginia, had told them of the government's decision to keep hunters and settlers out of the western lands. As they journeyed, they had had many discussions about the proclamation. Mostly they scoffed. Who would enforce such a law? How could such a long line zigzagging through the mountains be patrolled? Still they feared this might be their last hunt together. Since the country where they hunted was now officially Indian land, some of the tribes north of the Ohio River might move into the area to make sure the whites stayed out. But over and over again, the hunters raged that the British government favored the Indians over the whites when it came to western land. Empty land was for those who could take and hold and use it. Indians were well known as idlers.

Now Skaggs waded into the water with his horses and headed toward the islands. As the others followed, Walter Newman came striding up. He explained to Wallen that he and Cox had dropped behind to kill a huge rattler the dogs had found. Charles Cox, a kinsman of Wallen's, came sauntering along with his three dogs. He had the rattlesnake draped over the top of one of the horse packs. He brought it along for Old Man Blevins to boil down for oil. Snake oil was good for rheumatism, and William Blevins complained daily about his aching knees.

One of the dogs leaped on Wallen, and he twisted its ear playfully. He liked dogs but not on a hunt. They barked at the wrong time, scaring away game, or they were forever getting snake-bitten or wounded by bears. When he was after game, he wanted to concentrate on that, not on tending to hurt dogs. But Cox was a lackadaisical hunter, sometimes staying around the main campsite for weeks without firing a shot. Dogs were good company for him, as well as guards at night.

The three then began picking their way across the rocky ford. The water was shallow, hardly up to their knees in most places, and swift. The bottom was not slick, and they reached the western bank with no mishap. Here the path split. Newman and Cox took the branch to the right, which went through Hunter's Valley. Wallen checked the other path, which followed the Clinch, but found no signs of Indians. Then he hurried to catch up with the others.

The valley lay in shadow, but they might get another hour's traveling before stopping. Wallen was anxious to keep going as long as possible. It was the last week of October; November stared them in the face. By now he should have had a month's hunting behind him. It had taken him that wasted month to find two extra horses. Surely the delay would be worth it. Yesterday he had picked up from a stream a flat rock with a hole in it. Such a stone found in running water meant good luck to the finder. He would see if this was so on this long hunt.

Half-faced Shelter
and Long Rifle

The following day Wallen and his men left Hunter's Valley. For almost twenty years men had come to the narrow valley to kill game, and thus it had acquired its name and become known to the backwood settlers of Virginia and to the surveyors. It is called Hunter's Valley on today's maps.

From this point on, the men were in an area in which they had hunted and explored and which they had named as well. Name it and take it—that was Wallen's belief. Of all the names these men bestowed across the land where they hunted, only a few have survived and are in use today: Wallen Ridge, Wallen Creek, Newman Ridge, and Cox Branch.

None of the seven men on this expedition left a journal. Everything that is known about their hunts and their place names has survived through tradition. Tennessee's first historian, John Haywood, interviewed old pioneers to write his history in 1823. He says that Blackwater Creek and Greasy Rock Creek were also named by these men, and the names are still in use today. However, there was one stream known to Wallen's party that they named for a man whom they had never seen or known. They found "Powell" carved on so many beeches along its banks that they ungrudgingly let it be Powell River.

At the southern end of Hunter's Valley, the path turned westward toward Cumberland Gap. This in time would become the Wilderness Road. After only a couple of miles on this path, the hunters left it for the lower reaches of Blackwater Creek, a good twenty-five miles of rough travel to the south. There in a crook of Newman Ridge they made their main camp, or station camp as they termed it. Here they felt safe to leave their gear, horses, and skins, for, with no paths near, it was unlikely their camp would be discovered by Indians.

Each man picked a spot for his campsite. Then the packs were taken from the horses and the animals led off to graze. Some were hobbled at the edge of the brake to feed on cane leaves, and some staked in the meadow where the grass was thick and sweet. All the horses had bells tied about their necks. On the trail the clappers had been silenced by cloth wrapped around them. Now these cloths were removed. A straying horse was easier to find with a bell tinkling as it moved, and horses must be found. A successful hunt meant nothing if there were no horses to tote the skins out of the wilderness.

Pittman and Newman went off to hunt meat for supper. Jack Blevins gathered wood for a fire, while his father just sat chewing, his back against a log, his rheumatic legs stretched out in the warm afternoon sun. Skaggs cut saplings, which he would use to build a scaffold to hold his skins off the ground. Cox and the dogs wandered off down the creek bank.

Wallen was anxious to leave early the following morning, so he began to construct a half-faced shelter. A log was rolled into place at the rear of what would become the shelter. Then the sides were made of poles laid one on top of the other horizontally and held in place by upright stakes. These stakes were placed in pairs, two pairs in the front, two pairs in the back. The stakes in each pair were set only inches apart, to hold the poles in place, and thus two rough pole walls were constructed.

Next a crosspiece was set between the tops of the front pairs of stakes. Between these stakes Wallen laid long poles side by side, letting them slope down across the log to the ground at the rear. Over this pole roof he laid slabs of elm bark, weighted down with rocks. Later he would cover the roof with skins. All around the shelter he heaped dirt and moss up against the sides. With a fire burning at the open front, it would be warm in the shelter on even the coldest nights. Since he would spend so little time in the station camp, Wallen had constructed the simplest kind of half-faced shelter. He might have made one in which all three sides were of poles with a flat roof and high enough to walk around inside, but that was a lot of work and trouble. For now, he was content with this one.

Wallen sorted through his gear. He would leave his flitch of bacon, tied in a skin and suspended from a tree limb to keep it safe from marauding animals. But he'd take with him a wallet of corn meal and the packages of salt, red pepper, and sage. In the steady meat diet of the hunter, seasonings were important. Also he'd pack an extra rifle, bars of lead, powder, a three-legged skillet, an iron pot, a length of tow, and plenty of cloth patches for his rifle. The rifle parts, the hand vise and bellows for repair work, the horseshoes and nails, and other odds and ends he would leave under the half-faced shelter covered by a piece of linen duck.

The light was still good, so Wallen went off toward the bluffs of Newman Ridge to check the accuracy of his gun. Wallen, as well as the other six men, used a rifle, a fairly new weapon of their day. German and Swiss gunsmiths in Pennsylvania developed the rifle in the 1730's, perhaps earlier, in the region around Lancaster, though very little is known about this early rifle. But it was quite different from the rifle of Central Europe, which was short, heavy, hard to load, and accurate only at very short range, totally unfit for use in the woods of America.

The gunsmiths in Pennsylvania experimented until someone, whose name is unknown, devised a rifled-barreled gun with a small bore that weighed around ten pounds, much lighter than a musket. It used less powder and lead than other guns, yet it killed game at a hundred yards and farther, depending on the hunter. But the stroke of genius was the loading of the rifle with a greased cloth patch wrapped around the lead bullet.

In the European weapon the ball had to be hammered into the gun with a metal ramrod. This made it catch in the rifling, but it usually ruined the shape of the bullet. In the American gun the cloth patch engaged the rifle grooves and protected the shape of the lead ball, while a limber hickory rod was all that was needed to force the patch and bullet down onto the powder at the bottom of the barrel. The patch kept the ball from rolling out if the barrel was tilted downward.

Called a Pennsylvania rifle at first, it was the ideal weapon to shoot game or Indians. Without it there might not have been long hunters such as Wallen and those after him. By the end of the French and Indian War, it had come into general use along the frontier, and gunsmiths other than those in Pennsylvania were making rifles. It would in time become *the* gun going west with the settlers over the Wilderness Road. It would save Kentucky during the Revolutionary War and assume a new name—the Kentucky rifle.

Thomas Walker's party killed a great amount of game with their clumsy muskets and short-range carbines, not only because the woods teemed with animals but also because the bear and deer and buffalo were not frightened of men or used to being shot at. So Walker's men were able to get within close range of the game, where their weapons were the most effective.

By Wallen's time things were different. The animals were scarcer and much more alert. The hunter and the frontiersman no longer could get close to the game to shoot. Now he depended on a steady hand and a keen eye. Marksmanship had come to America with the long rifle, and with this tool and skill in its use he would conquer the continent.

Wallen found a beech that was suitable to his purpose. With his tomahawk he hacked off the bark on one side till it was smooth. In the middle of this white square, he made an X with mud for a target. From a good distance away, he fired several shots. Since the bullet marks were all clustered about the middle of the X, Wallen was satisfied that the rifle sights were set properly and the gun shot true. He then dug the battered bullets from the tree to be melted and remolded later. Lead was too precious to waste in this fashion.

Immediately after breakfast the next morning, Wallen placed his packs on two of his horses. When he had as many skins as two horses could carry, he would return to the station camp here, store his skins, and go out hunting again.

Wallen didn't like to wear leather in the woods. It was uncomfortable when wet. Brambles and vines made little whispering noises as they rubbed across leather, loud enough to disturb a deer as the hunter stalked it. Linsey-woolsey was best in the woods, and his shirt and knee-length pants were made of it. He had linsey leggings, too, which reached halfway up his thighs under his loose breeches and protected his legs. He had a tomahawk and knife in his belt; a shot pouch made of linen and a horn of powder were attached by separate thongs to a single leather strap looped over his left shoulder.

Most of Wallen's men were dressed as he was, though a few preferred tanned leather shirts or breeches. Skaggs had leather leggings. But all wore moccasins and floppy hats, as did Wallen.

The men discussed their plans, where they intended to hunt and how long they would be gone. They hunted singly, but at night usually two or three met to camp together. Wallen didn't care for company away from the main camp. All alone was the way he preferred. Telling them he was going to *his* mountain, he jerked on the lead line, and he and the horses left the station camp and headed west. The November sky was clear, the sun warm on his back. He held up the flat rock and looked through the hole. It was going to be a dandy long hunt.

3

A Crazy Buck Deer
and a Mad Stone

The great buck charged suddenly out of the bushes from one side with head lowered, its big antlers with their sharp prongs pointed straight at Wallen. The hunter swung around and raised his rifle, but there was no time to cock it. The buck was on him. Wallen leaped out of the way, feeling the horns scrape across his back.

The buck skidded to a stop, wheeled around, and was charging again by the time Wallen had his gun to his shoulder ready to fire. There was little to aim at but the top of the neck with a chance of hitting the vertebrae. He got off a fast shot, but the buck came on, slower this time, ready to swerve when the hunter did. Wallen grabbed his rifle by the barrel, and as the deer reached him, he sent the stock crashing into its muzzle. The buck halted, stunned, and stood shaking its head from side to side. Wallen swung his gun again and whopped it across the nose with all his strength, breaking the deer's jaw and splintering his wooden stock.

Dropping his rifle, Wallen snatched his butcher knife from the sheath at his side. He rushed forward, grabbed the buck around the neck, and slit its throat. Blood spouted from a severed artery over Wallen's breeches.

The buck leaped and turned and twisted, trying to dislodge the hunter, but Wallen held on and kept slashing at the lower part of the neck.

The buck fell to its knees. Wallen leaped away and stood there panting, watching the deer slowly slump over to its side. A long deep sigh and it was dead. November was the mating season for deer, and bucks were always crazy and wild then, but Wallen had never known one to attack a man before. He took dried grass and cleaned the blood from his hands and his knife handle, then set to work to skin the buck. It was his first skin on the hunt, and he hoped it was the last one he had to take in this fashion. Another such fight would do him in. Besides, making a gun stock took more time and trouble than molding bullets. Bullets were the proper thing for killing deer.

Wallen was quick at skinning—a stroke of the knife up the stomach from the tail to the neck, then a circling of the top of each leg and around the neck. "Snouts and shanks" had to be trimmed off or the hide wouldn't be acceptable for trading. With the skin clutched in his left hand, he pulled and cut it loose from the flesh.

He returned to his shelter under an overhanging shelf of rock on the side of Wallen Ridge. With such warm nights, there had been no need for him to waste time on another half-faced shelter. He had picked an ideal camping place. A spring flowed down the cliff into Wallen Creek several yards below. He had dammed up the spring and made a deep pool in which to soak his skins until he had time to scrape the hair and fat from them. Across the creek from his shelter was a meadow where the two horses grazed, close enough for him to hear the bells around their necks.

When he reached the bluff, he flung the buck skin into the soaking place. Then he got his second rifle out of his pack. It was an old one, and the barrel was a little worn and pitted, but it still shot true. This one had a different size bore from his broken one, so he had to mold new lead bullets for it. Rifles were not standardized, but were of different sizes and shapes. Even guns turned out by the same gunsmith varied from rifle to rifle. With lead balls molded and round patches cut from a length of cloth to wrap them in, Wallen was ready for the afternoon's hunt.

He cooked a piece of the buck's haunch for his dinner. Part of the rest he sliced up and put in a pot of water with seasoning. This would stew all afternoon and be ready on his return tonight. He also cut thin strips of meat and set them over a slow fire to smoke into jerk, or jerky as it was sometimes called. Meat preserved in this fashion kept a long time and would be on hand in case he had to leave for the station camp suddenly, or if he hunted far from his rock shelter and didn't want to return for meals. Finally he took his long-handled ax and chopped firewood.

Since Wallen hunted only deer for skins, the day's activity followed his daily pattern of existence. In the early mornings and late afternoons the deer fed, and Wallen, too, was out at those times, eager for a shot at one. During the middle of the day the deer rested, hidden among tall grasses along the creeks or in thickets away from heat and insects. At this time Wallen usually returned to his camp, not to rest, however. Scraping the hides was slow, hard work, and a hunter had to keep at this steadily so as not to get too far behind. There were other tasks also: cooking, mending clothes, keeping his gun clean and in working order, his knife and tomahawk sharp. Sometimes the horses gave trouble, or wolves or bears bothered his gear, and he had to find ways to protect his things from them.

By midafternoon he was out scouting around for sign of deer. He found a runway, an old one which had been used so much that it was more of a rut than a pathway. Deer are pretty much creatures of habit, and Wallen knew he could lie in wait here and have a chance to shoot plenty of deer before they became gun-shy and avoided the runway. But he saved it for another time. Right now he wanted to explore further.

Later he found a grove of white oaks. The nuts from these oaks are the sweetest of all acorns. The ground was littered with fallen acorns and pieces of shell and caps. There were fresh deer droppings all about the grove, so Wallen was sure the animals fed here and would return. Of course there might not be anything for the deer to eat if they stayed away too long, for the squirrels were everywhere gorging on the mast. He watched them for a while, then made himself as comfortable as he could, hidden among the roots of a poplar.

Time passed slowly. A few gnats were still about, and they flew around Wallen's head, but he was so used to the pests that he hardly noticed them. The squirrels squabbled and fussed. Jays called in the treetops, but no deer came. The sun had sunk behind Wallen Ridge, and the woods were shadowy. It would be tricky shooting in the half-light. He rose and stretched, preparing to go back to camp. Then there was scuffling in the leaves, followed by a great chattering of squirrels. The deer had arrived and chased the squirrels away.

Cautiously he peered around the poplar. There were eight does he could see among the trees eating, and a couple of very young bucks. Slowly he raised his rifle and held it against the trunk. He pulled back the hammer from safety, or half cock, to full cock, placed the sights on a deer's side, just behind the foreleg, and fired. The doe gave a jump and fell. The others stirred about uneasily but did not flee. One even went over to stare curiously at the fallen animal.

Behind the tree Wallen poured powder from his horn down the rifle barrel. Taking a patch, he held it over the end of the gun. He placed a lead ball on its center, pushed both into the barrel with his thumb, and shoved them down onto the powder with his hickory ramrod. He sprinkled powder in the frizzen pan, closed its cover, and once again cocked the piece.

Again he edged around the trunk, aimed, and fired. Another doe fell. Still the rest stayed to eat acorns. The sound of a rifle meant nothing to them because he was the first to hunt here, and they were not gun-shy. In all, Wallen downed five before the others finally became upset and fled. Now he set to work and skinned the animals. One doe still had most of its reddish summer coat; the others had shed theirs and had their winter pelts of slate-blue. As he worked, he ate a piece of raw liver, warm and bloody but delicious.

Finished at last, he sliced open all the does' stomachs and searched their contents. In one he found what he wanted. It was a honeycombed stone—a madstone, which could be placed on the bites of rabid animals to draw the poison out. It was always good to have one handy; any extra ones he could sell for a good price.

He cut a few choice collops of meat, leaving the rest for wolves, foxes, and opossums. There would be a great to-do there in the oak grove that night as they fought over the carcasses. They were welcome to the deer since he had what he wanted. He slung the hides over his shoulder and headed through the twilight for camp. Six skins he had taken today. It was a fine beginning.

4

A Tomahawked Panther

The days went quickly by, and the deerskins accumulated in the soaking pool. Wallen added the ashes from his fire to the pool daily. The wood ashes and water formed a lye, which loosened hair and made it easier to scrape off. Most of the hides were ready for dressing, but he had not worked on them because the days were so warm and pleasant, the hunting so fine, that he hated to be confined to camp.

One morning there was a smell of rain on the wind when Wallen rose. Overhead, scattered wispy clouds, tinged with the red sunrise, drifted across the sky, slowly moving together, an indication of bad weather ahead, Wallen knew. By the time he finished breakfast, there was an overcast, black and threatening. It would be a good day to work on the hides back under the cliff's ledge, where he would be dry when the rain began.

His scraping beam was a log wedged under a rock and placed across another in a slanting position. The bark had been cut from it and the rough spots smoothed with his ax. Selecting a skin from the pool, Wallen placed it over the upper end of the log. Sitting at the lower end, he began to scrape the pelt with a two-handled knife, pulling the blade toward him, removing the hair and the top layer of hide where the hair was rooted. Care had to be taken to keep the knife from going too deep and ruining the white skin underneath.

When he finished that side, he flipped the hide over and cut off the particles of meat and fat. If any of these were left, the hide would rot and also spoil the other skins.

The scraping done, he rinsed the skin in the creek and then squeezed the water from it. Looping it around a sapling, he pulled the hide back and forth, continuing this rubbing until it was dry and very soft. Now it was "half dressed." It could be handled and packed without harm and was acceptable for trading.

The rain held off through the morning. It got colder. Wallen worked steadily on the skins. When each was rubbed to softness, he folded it in half. Fifty of these he tied into a bale. This would weigh approximately a hundred pounds, and a horse carried two, one on each side. By afternoon a light rain began to fall. This soon turned to sleet and snow. The hunter stopped to cut a dead pine and drag it down the slope to his fire. It would be a cold night.

Then he went to look for his horses. He found them huddled close together at the edge of a canebrake, their manes stiff with ice, their backs white with snow. Unhobbling their front feet, he lead them back under a stand of huge hemlocks and tied them with a rope. They could move about with ease but not leave the protection of the trees. He fed them the last of their shelled corn and returned to camp.

During the night he was awakened by screams. He sat

up, flinging his blankets aside. The horses were in trouble. He had slept in his clothes. Quickly he put on his moccasins. Then grabbing his rifle and ammunition, he lit a pine knot torch in the fire and moved off down the slope. It was snowing hard, and the torch sputtered and spit. The bank was much too slippery to walk down, so he sat and slid to the creek. He started across and broke through the ice. The cold numbed his feet and legs, so that it pained him to move, but he struggled on toward the horses' fearful cries, half falling, half crawling up the slope.

Holding the torch high over his head, he moved in among the hemlocks. The horses continued to shriek, and now he could hear them thrashing about, thudding against the big tree butts and pawing the ground. Then he saw a shadowy figure stretched out along the ground, and as he neared, it turned, and the whiskered face of a panther was staring at him.

Clutching the torch and the rifle barrel in his left hand, Wallen placed the gun stock to his right shoulder. The flickering torch made aiming difficult, and the horses kept running back and forth in his line of fire, panic-stricken. Finally he fired. The cat squealed and leaped into the air. Again it crouched, caterwauling and lashing its tail.

The hunter reloaded, taking care not to drop the torch and keeping his eyes on the panther. The powder didn't pour readily, and he feared the dampness had gotten to it. He took careful aim and squeezed the trigger. The gun snapped, but there was no report. He cocked the weapon again and fired. The powder in the frizzen pan was too damp to ignite. One more time he tried, then put the rifle down.

The cat hadn't moved, but that didn't mean it was too badly hurt to charge. It might be waiting for him to move closer before it sprang at him. It would be after the horses the rest of the night, here or at the camp, Wallen knew. There were panthers who preferred horsemeat to any other, and this might be one of them. He had to kill it.

Slipping his tomahawk from his belt, he moved toward the cat, circling for a throw at the neck. The panther swung around with him, snarling and growling, its eyes slitted. The torch was burning out, so Wallen had to hurry. He took a step forward and flung the tomahawk with all his might. There was a heavy thud, and the blade sank into the panther's head. It screeched and tensed to spring forward. Wallen drew out his knife. But the cat went suddenly limp and slumped to the ground. It was dead, a good riddance for the hunting lands. The hunter hurriedly collected his weapons and in the fading light of the torch led the horses to his rock shelter.

He slept peacefully the rest of the night. He didn't worry too much about the many dangers to himself or the horses all around him in the wilderness. He had his rifle. Much could go wrong with it, as had happened this night—damp powder, a dull flint, a grain of dust in the touchhole. No matter how careful a hunter was, sometimes such things happened, and then his rifle was useless.

In such cases he could rely on his tomahawk or his knife. Even his two hands and his wits could serve a strong and resourceful man. Elisha Wallen was such a man, and he had no bad dreams.

Wallen had to move his camp every seven or eight days, for by that time the deer and other game had become gun-shy and hunting became difficult. With every move he assured himself of a fresh supply of skins and food. The long hunter liked to eat, and the fall wilderness provided him with a plentiful variety. Bear meat, fat and sweet. Bear feet roasted in hot ashes. Roast goose, squirrel fried in bear's oil, tender beaver tails baked in wet oak leaves in embers all night. When cornmeal gave out, the white dry breast of the turkey was a fine substitute for bread. Then there was buffalo to provide delicious hump fleece, tongue, and marrow bones. To supplement a meat and fowl diet, hickory and beech nuts were eaten, as well as walnuts, sweet, juicy persimmons, tart fox grapes, and crunchy crab apples chilled by the early frosts.

He worked his way, camp by camp, slowly down Wallen Creek, and by late December he had two hundred half-dressed skins. These were tied into bales and, one bright, cold day, loaded on his horses. The time had come to set out for the main station camp to store his skins and visit a while with the other hunters. Leading his animals and whistling the British ballad of the "Three Ravens," he headed eastward, satisfied with the hunting.

5

Long Hunters and
Tall Tales

The sun broke through the clouds as Wallen went through the gap in Newman Ridge. But it was a winter sun, weak and pale. By the time he reached the station camp on Blackwater Creek, the sun had disappeared again, and the sky was dark gray. There had been a heavy frost that morning. Clouds on frost meant severe weather.

The long hunter found Old Man Blevins sitting by the fire, chewing tobacco and stirring a pot of stew. His father-in-law eyed the bales of skins and said the hunting must have been fine—two fully loaded horses and back before the others. Wallen nodded. Hunting had been good, better than usual for him, though he had had a little trouble with a buck deer and with a panther that had decided horsemeat would make a tasty meal.

Blevins said he'd been bothered some by wolves, but he had killed one and wounded another, and after that they left him alone.

Wallen unloaded, fed his horses, and checked on the animals he had left behind. Then he commenced to cut saplings for a platform on which to store his skins. With a covering of elk hides and bearskins, they would be protected from the damp and high enough from the ground to keep animals from bothering them.

Skaggs returned to the camp a couple of days later. He, like Wallen, preferred to hunt alone. He hadn't yet been ready to come back to the base camp, but his horse had cast a shoe, and the tools for replacing it were all here. After shoeing his horse, he joined the other two around the fire. He had something he was eager to tell. He had found a strange spring of water. The water bubbled up out of a hole in the ground at certain times, and later just as suddenly disappeared into the earth.

Wallen said it was an ebb and flow spring and he had seen one once. When rocks were thrown into it, the spring spit them up. It spit worse than his tobacco-chewing father-in-law.

The weather turned bitter cold as Wallen had predicted, and there was some snow. Blevins worried about his son, for young Blevins had brought with him a bag of camphor and skunk oil to wear around his neck to ward off the boll hives and other throat ailments, and he had left it behind.

Pittman and Newman arrived next. They had spent most of their time hunting bears and boiling down the fat into oil. Newman liked to begin the day with a big drink of bear oil. He claimed it not only made him feel warm inside, but it also made his shooting eye keener. Bears had already given up eating mast and begun to hibernate, and this had been the last chance to get them—and the smoked hams and oil they provided.

Pittman said they had hunted along a creek where they had never been before and that they had a favorite spot to drink, a rock that sloped down the bank into the stream. Their clothes were very greasy from handling the bear meat, and the rock soon became greasy also, from their constant lying on it to drink. So they had named the stream Greasy Rock Creek.

Wallen liked to know where streams were located, the route of paths, mountain passes, and prominent knobs and peaks, for then he could picture the face of the country in his mind. Such a map sense was essential for a long hunter wandering the woods and might well save his life sometime. Newman drew in the dirt, showing how Greasy Rock Creek flowed southeastward into the Holston River, and Wallen studied the map carefully.

Thus the days and nights passed with the long hunters spending most of their time eating and talking around the fire. Skaggs had trapped a beaver with only half a tail. Newman showed a rock that was gold-speckled and unnaturally heavy. Wallen told of finding a pair of shed elk antlers so tall that he could walk under them without stooping.

Old Man Blevins snorted. If his son-in-law was going to lie, he might as well lie, too. He remembered once finding a hollow tree that acted in a mighty strange way. It grew big and then shrank, puffed out big, then grew small. He figured it might be the devil inside, so he cut the tree down and out came two dozen or so raccoons. He was so surprised that he let them all get away without killing a one. They must have been packed so tight in the hollow tree that when they breathed in, the tree swelled. When they let their breath out, the tree would shrink.

Pittman had seen a hollow sycamore so big that he stabled his horses in it. The only trouble was they kept getting out through the knotholes and running away.

When the tall tales gave out, they argued about the weather—whether thick corn husks foretold a hard winter, whether a man could predict weather with the breastbone of a goose killed in the fall. Then one day young Blevins and Cox and his dogs turned up, and the old man was relieved to see that his son hadn't caught the croup or been laid low by the throat thrush.

Blevins flung down a piece of bloody skin with a tuft of hair on it. There was a string of glass beads in the upright patch of hair. It was a scalp, the young man informed them, taken from a Cherokee, the best kind of Cherokee—a dead one!

His father grunted. He shouldn't have taken it, Skaggs said, for scalps were thin and scrawny this time of year and not worth bothering with. The hunters laughed, and Newman pointed out that the days of paying bounty money for scalps were over, so what good was it?

Jack Blevins wanted to show it back home to a fellow who was always bragging about his take of scalps, yet never had he had one to prove his prowess in killing Indians. This scalp might shut him up, and it would be a great trophy to give to his squeamish sisters.

Cox said if it hadn't been for his dogs, the Indian might likely have killed one of them. The red man was skulking about their camp when the dogs picked up his scent and routed him out of the bushes. The dogs also treed a panther, which Cox shot. Cox teased Wallen by saying that all hunters should take dogs into the woods with them to help them in dangerous situations. Wallen told him that he had had a bit of panther trouble, too, but he had handled it all by himself and felt he could continue to do so in the future. He grinned and added that he hated to see a hunter too lazy to do his own fighting.

After a few days Wallen tired of talk and inactivity. He packed his gear and headed west for Powell River to take more deerskins. Soon after, the others went their separate ways, and the long hunt went on.

6

The Trail of No Return

It is safe to say that in the early years of the 1760's, Wallen and his companions hunted over the territory between the Clinch and Holston Rivers and the Cumberland Mountains in what is now westernmost Virginia and a part of eastern Tennessee. This is the area in which many of the creeks and mountains still bear their names or names traditionally bestowed by those men. And it was in this area, not far from Cumberland Gap and close to Wallen Ridge, that Elisha Wallen settled when he left his home in Virginia.

However, since these early hunters left no written records, it is nearly impossible to guess how much farther beyond this region they roamed or the exact dates of their long hunts. As they were after game and game went everywhere, they may have gone farther west than historians have credited them.

They might well have reached the game-choked lands of central Kentucky and middle Tennessee. No Indians lived there, but for some time this had been the hunting territory of the numerous tribes north of the Ohio River and for the scattered southern Indian nations. However, in the 1760's all these Indians were too unorganized and

too weak from years of warfare to threaten any tres-
passers. Only a hunter's whims or fancies might prevent
him from wandering as far west as he liked.

Wallen and his friends were among the first of those
men who were in later times to become known as "long
hunters." They went into the forest for months, a year at
a time. They reaped its bumper crop of skins and furs
and meat. And in the shadows under the great trees,
they were changing into a new and different kind of man,
an American who was unlike Doctor Thomas Walker and
his peers.

Walker went into the wilderness to explore and hunted
along the way. Wallen and his men went to hunt and explored along the way. The difference was much greater
than might be expected, and it had taken place in a short
span of time. Walker went into the unknown. Wallen went
into country he had never seen before, but which he knew
well enough, for it was like country he had seen and
hunted over for years. Walker hoped the forest would sus-
tain him on his journey. Wallen expected it not only to
keep him alive but also to provide him with a livelihood.
Walker hardly knew what to anticipate from animals, Indians, weather. Wallen not only knew what to anticipate; he figured he knew also how to handle anything that
came up.

In the seaboard cities of the east, the long hunters were
generally referred to as "woodsmen," though quite often
they were called "white Indians" and held in contempt.
They had indeed adopted many of the Indian's ways, for
that was how they would conquer the wilderness. But
they were not Indians. They were becoming something

never seen in the world before—the Frontiersman, the Pioneer American.

When a hunter like Wallen went into the woods, he was prepared not simply to collect skins to make money. He was prepared to be his own cook, geographer, tailor, cobbler, carpenter, doctor, housekeeper, gun repairman, tinker, soldier, or to take up any other trade that the situation demanded. He didn't take with him a great deal of equipment, only the most essential and simple tools, but he made do with those. If he lost his gear, he philosophically used whatever the woods around him had to offer and continued on his way.

It was easy enough for him to shoot a long rifle twice in a minute. It took no great exertion to make himself a suit of clothes or a dwelling from animal skins. He could throw a tomahawk as effortlessly as breathing, fight a rattlesnake barehanded, skin any kind of beast with a knife, a gun flint, or a sliver of cane, and hear an Indian blink in the brush five miles away.

The woods had become a way of life. The skills, the clothing, the habits of the woodsman were very different from those of farmer or townsman. Even his language was full of terms with a forest flavor: "to make tracks," "play possum," "shoot for the hump," or be "a flash in the pan." He wore no fringed hunting shirt or coonskin cap, but he was thinking about it. His rifle and his ax were not yet the extensions of himself they were to become, but they were already indispensable to him. He was, as he had to be, stronger, tougher, lonelier, and warier than his more civilized brothers.

Tradition says that Wallen led three great long hunts

and that on his first one, in 1761, there were eighteen men with him, and they stayed in the wilderness for eighteen months. During such a lengthy period, they must have explored farther than we will ever know for sure, following game farther and farther over the mountains, across the fresh green landscape that stretched endlessly and invitingly before them. But the hardships and solitariness of such a long hunt must have driven them even farther, down a trail they would never follow back, away from Europe and toward America.

NEWSCAST OF 1774

Much about the new western land of Kentucke
and its hold on
American imagination and reality

KENTA-KE

The year begins with a new word that almost makes the
Americans forget their troubles with Britain, her domi-
neering ways and her tax assessments. The word is Kentucke—a novel name for the great green spaces west of
the Appalachian Mountains. There seem to be as many
ways to pronounce it as there are variants in its spelling:
Caintuck, Kantucqui, Cantucky, to mention a few. White
traders among the Indian tribes have known and used the
word for some time, saying it comes from an Iroquois
word, Kenta-ke, which means "place of the fields" or
"meadows."

It is strange that for more than two decades travelers
have visited Kentucke and returned to the eastern settlements with stories about it, yet it has remained till recent
times a dark and unexplored land. Long ago traders reported on the sweetness of the many springs and rivers;
hunters extolled the abundance and variety of woodland
trees and game; and curious sightseers came home with

tales of mammoth caves and strange creatures and giant bleached bones. Still, only now has it come to be believed that Kentucke is the richest land in America, that it is indeed an earthly paradise, a Canaan of milk and honey. Today it is well known that Kentucke lies empty, waiting the ax, the rifle, and the cabin.

A GREAT BUZZ

What a great buzz Kentucke has created among Americans. Though little enough is known about the true nature of this western country, it seems already to have become the repository for American dreams and hopes for the future. Before the winter snows melt and the cold ends this year, surveyors are on their way to the western lands. Settlers are not far behind them. By March James Harrod and his followers lay out the first town in Kentucke, build cabins, and name it Harrodstown, or as it was later called, Harrodsburg. Town lots are distributed by raffle. At the same time others are roaming across Kentucke and staking out land claims by the old method of tomahawk rights—cutting their initials on trees along the boundary lines of their plots.

A plague of "Kentucke rash" has broken out among the white people, and the pestilence is spreading among the land-hungry east of the Appalachians. Many are wary of all this activity and believe Kentucke is not worth the risk of another Indian war. Two powerful tribes claim Kentucke as their own hunting land, the Shawnee and the Cherokee. It is believed these Indians are willing to take up the war hatchet to stop white encroachment onto these grounds. Other Americans scoff at the idea of any serious threat from the Indians. They are asking what right either tribe has to Kentucke.

THE WANDERING SHAWNEE

On early French maps, the Shawnee were called Chaou-anons, and the river where their towns were located was given their name. This is the same river that Doctor Thomas Walker labeled Cumberland. LaSalle reported finding Chaouanons west of the Mississippi River. Early English narratives of South Carolina mentioned a warring tribe living upcountry from Charles Town on a large river. These Indians lived there only a short while, but the river was named for them—the Savannah, another name for Shawnee. In Pennsylvania, where a Shawnee group once resided only a short time, they were known as Sawano.

In the 1740's a wandering band of Shawnee established a trading town on the Warrior's Path in Kentucke. It was called Es-kip-pa-kith-i-ka and lasted only a short while. For a great number of years now, most of the Shawnee have lived along the Scioto River north of the Ohio. But who knows, perhaps in ancient times there were many Shawnee towns in Kentucke? Certainly the tribe has long claimed ownership of this land.

The Shawnee fought on the losing side in the French and Indian War and today can expect no help from their former ally. Only their kinsmen, the Delaware, and remnants of other northern tribes stand ready to help the Shawnee hold Kentucke, if they choose to try to do so.

CHEROKEE MOUNTAINEERS

Far to the south of the Shawnee live the Cherokee. Back
in dim antiquity, the Cherokee say that their grandfa-
thers migrated from the northwest to the lower end of
the Appalachian Mountains. There they found the valleys occupied by a "moon-eyed" race. These "wretches"
they drove away. Then the Cherokee settled among the
mountains and have been there ever since.

Today their towns are grouped in four separate com-
munities, yet the Cherokee consider themselves one nation. They farm and hunt and only move their townsites
when the soil around them ceases to produce. They are a
large and powerful nation and stand squarely in the way
of any white advance down the Great Valley from Virginia, or west from North and South Carolina. The British have taken away much of their land over the years by
treaties. Yet the Cherokee still have Kentucke, which
they claim is entirely theirs, that they took it long ago
from the Shawnee by defeating them in battle and driving
them from the country.

Can the Cherokee hope to hold Kentucke against the
whites? They live farther away from that hunting land
than do the Shawnee. This is a great disadvantage. The
Cherokee have been killing any white intruders they have
found in Kentucke, however. It is enough to make any
white man pause and think before bringing his family into
that country.

THE RED PINCHERS

The westernmost settlement in Virginia is along the
Clinch River. As spring begins, these frontiersmen are

worried. They know that peace parties are traveling
back and forth constantly between the Ohio country of the
Shawnee and the Cherokee towns. Although the Cherokee and Shawnee have been enemies since ancient times, it
seems as if they might now unite to resist the whites in
Kentucke. If this comes about, Clinch River settlers realize they will be caught between the Shawnee north of
them and the Cherokee to the south.

Those settlers living along the Watauga River, the
southernmost outposts, will be pinched in this vise, too.
Not only are they within sixty miles of the nearest Cherokee towns, but they are also under the protection of neither Virginia nor North Carolina. They are on their own
on land leased from the Cherokee two years ago. The red
pinchers will squeeze them to death along with their
Clinch River neighbors. What should they do?

THE CHEROKEE BILLEY POWDER KEG

The Wataugans have never had trouble with the Indians.
Now the British Superintendent of Indian Affairs says
the Cherokee were cheated out of their land and that
the Wataugans must leave at once. As small and as iso-
lated as the Watauga settlement is, it has to depend on
friendliness with the Cherokee to survive. Indians do not
always listen to the words of their British agent. Would
the Cherokees be interested in more payments and a re-
newal of the land lease?

No one knows, but it is worth a try. This April the
Wataugans invite the Cherokee to a business session with
a barbecue, horse races, and other entertainments to follow. The Indians accept, and all is going well between the

races when a white outsider named Crabtree murders a brave called Cherokee Billey. Crabtree had been heading for Kentucke in 1773 with the William Russell-Daniel Boone settlement party when Indians attacked. The oldest sons of Russell and of Boone were tortured and killed, and Crabtree barely escaped. He swore vengeance to all red men.

After Cherokee Billey's murder, the Indians leave, and the Wataugans fear for the worst. Many begin to pack their possessions. War is bound to come now. Nevertheless, Watauga sends peace emissaries to the Cherokee towns.

DUNMORE'S WAR YIELDS KENTUCKE

The end of April brings another Indian murder, this time in the Ohio country. The victims are the family of a Shawnee chief named Logan. He takes the warpath. Forts are begun along the Clinch River, powder and ammunition stored. Daniel Boone and Michael Stoner, two hunters familiar with Kentucke, are sent to warn the Virginia surveyors and other white men there.

By July the Wataugans breathe more easily—the Cherokee are pacified. But Governor Dunmore of Virginia issues a call for troops among the borderers. He is weary of constant trouble from the Shawnee. Watauga and Clinch River settlements send men to help subdue the northern Indians. However, it is not until early October that the white army meets and crushes the Shawnee and their Indian allies at Point Pleasant on the Ohio River. Dunmore's War is over. In the peace that ensues, the

Shawnee agree to give up Kentucke and never go there. From Pennsylvania to South Carolina, frontiersmen are jubilant. Kentucke is practically theirs—if something could only be done about the Cherokee and their ridiculous claim of ownership.

EXPECT THE UNEXPECTED

As 1774 comes to an end, rumors along the border say that a land company has been formed and that it is going to buy Kentucke from the Cherokee. This rumor becomes fact as Richard Henderson of North Carolina travels through the Watauga region, returning from a conference with the Cherokee headmen. His company is treating with the Cherokee in March of the following year. What can this mean to the future of the borderers and to Kentucke? No one knows. But once again the frontiersmen have learned to expect the unexpected and to realize that change is the ordinary rule of their lives. Now, along the frontier, eyes and ears are turned for any news from Sycamore Shoals, where Henderson's company is going to meet with the Cherokee kings.

PART THREE

DANIEL BOONE
Hero—Super American

I

Some Pumpkin!

The Watauga River banks were lined with giant syca-
mores. Their upper branches were bare and bleached as
old bones, but the twigs were beginning to swell with
buds. The sun shone, but it was cold under the trees where
Daniel Boone stood idly gazing out over the rocks and
white roiling water. He had once waded across Sycamore
Shoals to the island yonder to hide from Cherokee Indians. That had been a good number of years ago when
this country was still wild and unsettled and Boone was
living across the mountains in North Carolina.

There was a shriek behind him. He turned to see a tiny
naked Indian boy running through the trees. Two bigger
boys were chasing him. As he dashed past Boone, he
tripped on a root and fell hard. His breath went shoosh-
ing out of him. The hunter laid down his rifle and picked
up the child and slapped him on the back till he caught his
breath again.

The other two boys watched, and when the younger
child had recovered, they seized him and led him away.
He was their prisoner of war and had escaped. They
were going to burn him at the stake. The prisoner twisted

and struggled in vain. The two older children marched him away.

Boone smiled. Children, red or white, liked to play war. Even the children of the peace-loving Society of Friends had war games when their parents weren't around. As a young boy in Pennsylvania, he and other Quaker youngsters had enjoyed many a mock battle among themselves and with Indian boys.

It was like a Quaker gathering today at Sycamore Shoals, with the Cherokee and the frontiersmen eating and talking together in such friendly fashion. Horse-swapping, a dangerous business anytime, had been taking place between the Indians and the white men, and so far no one had complained of being cheated and no blood had been spilled.

This treaty was certainly a marvel. Who would have expected that Kentucke could be bought, or that it could be bought so cheaply? It had taken a man of shrewdness and much legal knowledge to realize how and when the Indians could be approached on the subject of selling their hunting lands. And it had taken a man of boldness to seize the opportunity when it came along. Such a man was Richard Henderson.

The Louisa Company had been organized by Henderson and four other North Carolinians in the summer of 1774. Its purpose was, as their prospectus said, "to rent or purchase a certain Territory lying on the west side of the mountains on the waters of the Mississippi from the Indian tribes now in possession thereof." By the start of the new year, the company had been reorganized, three new members taken into it, and the name changed to the

Transylvania Company. Henderson was head of it, and he and the Cherokee chief, Attakullakulla, had agreed to meet in early March, 1775, at Sycamore Shoals to begin the formal negotiations for the sale of Kentucke.

It was the ninth of March, and still the treaty talks had not begun. Boone wished Henderson would get on with it. Already he had advertised that the company had land for sale in Kentucke, though the deeds were not yet signed nor the cabin full of goods paid to the Cherokee.

Boone had left his axmen at the Big Island, and they were as anxious to get going to Kentucke as he was. Henderson had told him to hire enough men to widen the route so that wagons might travel over it to Kentucke. Boone had thirty men, but he didn't believe twice that number could make the roadway good enough for wagons. It was rough country, and shanks' mare and horses had been the only means of reaching the western lands up to now. Wagons! It'd take a stubborn, patient man to try to drive a wagon to Kentucke.

Daniel picked up his rifle. He still had to find his brother, Squire, and make sure he had gotten those extra axes. He wandered off through the trees. There were campfires everywhere. Some people said many of the Cherokees had arrived for the treaty as long ago as January. There were a great number here now, maybe a thousand. Who could tell—they shifted their camps and drifted in and out so much. However many there were, Boone had never seen this many Indians gathered together in his life. It was a wonder to see former enemies like this, dressed in their most colorful clothes—ruffled shirts and satin breeches, armbands and hair ribbons, silver medals about their necks, ear dangles and bracelets. No one was in war paint, and few bore arms.

The Indians liked a festival, a party—there was no doubt about it. Even the women, who were seldom caught smiling in their towns, were now laughing and giggling and in the gayest of moods. Boone passed a campfire where some men played cane flutes and others danced. Beyond them three men were shooting darts through their blowpipes but were having trouble hitting the single target propped against a stump. The darts were tipped with milkweed down and were being blown every which way by the wind. One dart was hit by a gust of wind and swerved off to strike an Indian woman bending over a pot. The men laughed heartily, and the woman stamped off angrily.

What a contrast to pass from where the Indians played and joked to where groups of whites sat around a fire seriously discussing land. Everyone wanted a parcel of Kentucke and speculated on how much the Transylvania Company would ask per acre, what kind of crops would grow best there, how long the journey to Kentucke might take, and so on. No one talked of anything else. Daniel grinned. Why should they? It was like no other place. It was true, as his friend Michael Stoner said, Kentucke was some pumpkin!

One of William Bean's boys raced up to tell Boone that Henderson wanted to see him. The hunter hurried toward the cabin filled with trading goods and found Judge Henderson standing at the cooking fire, where halves of bear and beef and deer roasted on racks, turkeys and geese on spits. Beside Henderson stood Attakullakulla, one of the most powerful of the Cherokee headmen. The Indian was tiny, his face scarred and wrinkled. He greeted Boone warmly, for they had met many times before.

Henderson said they waited for a few more Cherokee chiefs to arrive before the treaty discussions began. But Attakullakulla assured him there would be no hitch in the proceedings. All the Cherokee were in favor of selling their rights to Kentucke. Henderson saw no reason why Boone shouldn't start blazing the roadway at once.

This was welcome news, and Boone rounded up his brother and Stoner and several other of the axmen and left immediately for the Big Island.

2

Road to Paradise

The Big or Long Island extends for about five miles in
the South Fork of the Holston River. It was a revered
spot to the Cherokee, and they kept possession of it until
1806, at which time it was ceded to the United States.
On the morning of March 10, 1775, the island seemed to
float on the dark river in the fog. Only the water was noisy
as it tumbled past. Upstream a loon called.

Opposite the lower end of the island and on the north
bank, Boone waited for the rest of his party. The night's
fires were out, the horses loaded, and the axes sharp-
ened. He was impatient to be away. The missing axmen
had camped upstream but had promised to turn up early.
The loon sounded again, and before its loud call was
ended, it had been drowned out by singing:

> "Lord Bonnie, he was a hunting man
> And a-hunting he did ride
> With a hunting horn all around his neck
> And his sword by his side."

Boone laughed aloud. He had bargained for axmen,
not singers, and the chorus was more like wolf-howling

than music. Still, singing eased back-breaking work and whiled away the time. Many a lonely day in the wilderness had passed more easily and quickly with the aid of song.

The songsters were seven young men from Rutherford County, North Carolina, who had set out from home for Kentucke for adventure and a chance to see the land they had heard so much about. Felix Walker, one of the youths, wrote an account of this journey when he was an old man. He said that none of the seven had any experience in traveling through the woods, but they had placed themselves in the hands of an expert woodsman, a Captain William Twitty.

Boone didn't need woodsmen. He wanted hard workers who could stand a long day of steady chopping. Twitty pointed out that these young men came from farms, were used to hard work, and could handle an ax. Boone had hired them as well as Twitty. Now he was prepared to push them on the road work, for he wanted to reach Kentucke as soon as possible and begin a fort. Henderson expected one built by the time of his arrival next month.

After greeting the newcomers, Boone began to organize the group. Some of the men he sent off at once with his friend, Benjamin Cutbirth. With hatchets and tomahawks, they were to clear away the brush and saplings along the sides of the trace. His brother, Squire, was placed in charge of the main group with felling axes. They were to follow the others and chop down the large trees. Still others he told to care for the riding and pack horses.

Then Boone went on ahead to blaze the trees that

would point out the way the road was to follow. Michael Stoner was with him. Both frontiersmen went armed and were on the lookout for game.

Felix Walker's narrative is short on details. Only a few of the thirty with Boone are named. In one sentence Walker takes them from Long Island to Kentucke, names a few of the rivers and mountains crossed, and mentions the killing of a bear, which was eaten for supper. However, the narrative expresses the emotions of Walker and his youthful friends at their departure, and surely they must have been the same for many another traveler to Kentucke before this time and after.

". . . perhaps no adventurers since the days of Don Quixote, or before, ever felt so cheerful and elated in prospect; every heart abounded with joy and excitement in anticipating the new things we could see, and the romantic scenes through which we must pass; and, exclusive of the novelty of the journey, the advantages and accumulations ensuing on the settlement of a new country was a dazzling object with many of our company. Under the influence of these impressions we went our way rejoicing . . ."

The wilderness was no longer a beast to be chastened and chained. It was a dazzling possession—a precious thing to be held in the hand. The road ahead of these axmen, though not yet even projected, led straight to paradise.

3

Troublesome Creek and
a Grave Visited

When Boone and his axmen left Long Island and headed north, there was little work to be done, for they followed a well-worn wagon road. The young men from North Carolina were in high spirits. They joked and sang and played tricks on each other. Captain Twitty had brought with him a big bulldog, and these young adventurers whiled away many hours trying to make friends with this animal. But the dog was a serious-minded creature and would not be distracted from his duty, which was to walk beside Captain Twitty and guard him as they made their way through the woods.

They chopped little and traveled fast, but Boone hustled them along even faster, for he well knew that a good part of the path ahead would be much more difficult, and there would be times when their progress would be measured in rods and not miles.

Still such high jinks and fun were infectious, especially to Boone, who was himself a lively and good-natured man. He gave in often to their plea to tell stories of his hunting and trapping days, of his friendships with various Indians, for Boone knew and liked and understood the red men and their way of life. He had sat around campfires with them and traveled with them on the trails.

And Boone, in turn, liked to listen to Cutbirth talk of his own exploits, for Cutbirth had journeyed west to the banks of the awesome Mississippi River. Boone planned to cross west of that river himself some day. One of the youths in Captain Twitty's group was convinced that on the other side there was nothing but black desert, falling deeper and deeper into the earth, and some of the others seemed to think it might not be a safe place to explore.

Near Moccasin Gap the party left the wagon road. Now they must really set to work, for though a trail was here, it was hard to follow, the way was narrow and overgrown, and it took real chopping and hacking to clear away the trees and undergrowth and make the path plain to see and easy to follow.

The pace slowed even more as they went through the gap and turned west to cut the road along Moccasin Creek, a route seldom used but known by the Clinch River settlers. By afternoon they were working along a creek which, Boone said, had no name. It flowed through a gorge so narrow that often the trail had no place to go except down the rocky bed of the stream itself. The going was slow and rough; rocks and fallen trees and driftwood barred the way constantly. There was no time to look about, and perhaps only Boone marked the blooming sarvisberry and plum trees with their white tracings on the steep hillsides, or the yellow violets and bluets opening in the rock crevices, and the other signs of spring on its way. Boone was one of those men who loved the woods for their own sake, who delighted in their solitude and beauty, and he had a keen eye for such things.

By dark of that day, they arrived on the banks of the

Clinch River, worn out and dirty and bedraggled—and they had a name for that stream which had tormented them so—Troublesome Creek.

The route Boone had selected from Moccasin Gap to the Clinch River was almost a straight line westward. Frontiersmen, like the Indians generally, preferred a straight and direct line between two points. Even if it meant climbing a mountain or traveling a creek bed, they preferred to go forward boldly, following a beeline.

Moccasins, as someone has said, are simply a decent way of going barefoot, but they were for the most part all the footgear the pioneers had for traveling. They favored keeping them dry if possible, for the process of drying and softing them was troublesome. Yet the woodsmen didn't like to swerve from a course even to avoid wading. There was an easier, less watery way through the Clinch Mountains north of the route Boone had chosen, but it was more roundabout, and he rejected it.

By sunrise the next morning, Boone had his party fording the Clinch River. It was an easy ford in low water, along a ledge of rock partly out of water. But spring floods made it more difficult. However, all the axmen crossed the way they liked to—safe and dry-shod on horseback and with no mishaps.

Boone was now in territory that he knew thoroughly. The previous year he had been in charge of forts in the Clinch River valley during Dunmore's War against the Shawnee. Boone had hunted these surrounding mountains, scouted the valleys for marauding Indians, and had traversed the country many times before that as he had explored westward.

But he realized that being in familiar country was no

protection against trouble. Two of the men had a quarrel over a missing ax. One of the young men was nervous about snakes, and when he spotted one lying on a log across the trail, he turned so quickly to run away from it that he wrenched his ankle. There were cuts and bruises to be treated, also, and some of the overworked men complained of feeling feverish.

Daniel often gathered herbs and simples to make a tea, which he urged on them at bedtime to relax them after a hard day's work. Other aromatic and refreshing herbs he used to give the men a lift in the middle of the day. But otherwise he left the doctoring to his brother Squire who, Daniel believed, was as successful in treating patients with various woodsy items as an educated doctor with his pills and calomel.

Squire not only knew how to expel intestinal worms, but he also knew various astringents as well as powerful teas and infusions for the ailing. He stopped blood flowing from a cut with spider webs, he dusted wounds with the powder from dry puffballs to guard against infection, and for the ague he brewed a tea of such nastiness that the mere smell was said to work a cure.

One afternoon Daniel took his rifle and left the others. Many of the young men hoped he had gone to shoot a buffalo for their supper, for they had never tasted the meat. But Boone wasn't hunting. Squire and Stoner and Cutbirth knew where he was headed. Ahead lay the grave of Daniel's oldest son, and he always visited it when he could, to make sure no wolves or Indians had violated it.

In the fall of 1773, Boone and William Russell, the leading pioneer of the Clinch River valley, had joined forces to make a first settlement of Kentucky. Boone, and those going with him from North Carolina, sold their farms and personal possessions. They wouldn't be returning, for they hoped paradise would be their home henceforth. Women, children, livestock, and riflemen joined Russell's group in the Clinch valley, and all headed on west. However, difficulties arose, and the large group ended up split into three separate traveling sections. Russell's and Boone's sons, with some others, were the middle party and were hurrying to catch up with those ahead under Daniel's captaincy. Night caught them about three miles from the leaders, though the boys didn't know they were so close. They camped. At daybreak Shawnee and Cherokee attacked. The boys were captured and tortured slowly to death. Russell and Boone buried their sons at the scene of their murders on the head of Wallen Creek. Boone, in spite of his grief, had been willing to continue the journey, but the others were too disheartened, and in the end they all returned to the Clinch River settlements.

Boone found the double grave still covered with rocks and logs. He was satisfied the boys' bodies were untouched. Jamie had been his eldest son. From the time he was a toddler, he had shared his father's love for the wild, going with Daniel on expeditions when he was too young to walk such distances and had to be carried inside Boone's shirt.

Slipping quietly back, Boone continued blazing trees to show the axmen where he wanted the road to go. Once again he was trying to settle Kentucke. Could he and his men, with Henderson's help, hold paradise this time? Or had Jamie died in vain, in attempting to realize a dream that would never be anything but a nightmare?

4

The Red Serpent
in Paradise

Several days later the axmen were resting in the saddle of
Cumberland Gap. Since their route down Powell Valley
had been over rolling land and the clearing work had
been easy, Boone now urged the party to hurry through
the gap. Cumberland River lay ahead, and the heavy
wooded hills and thick canebrakes beyond would bring
the hardest work they would encounter. It was best to get
at it.

But those whose first time it was to view this famous
mountain passageway wanted to linger. Cumberland Gap
—the gateway to the land of hopes and opportunity and
marvels! How often they had heard of it back home!
Men spoke of Cumberland Gap as if it were some myth-
ical place in western mists. And here they were in the very
gap itself. So now they were relishing their visit. They
were sightseeing, like any tourist, gawking at the high
cliffs overhead, climbing fallen rocks for a better view,
and poking about here and there. A few examined the
many initials cut in the trunks of trees and tried to guess
the names of the carvers.

Someone asked if Boone had carved his name here.
Stoner teased him about how, whenever Boone killed a

bear or a turkey or stomped out a fire, he always carved his name and his exploits on the nearest tree. Boone snorted and replied that he had cut no name on these trunks. He left his mark only deep in the wilderness, where no other had been before. Too many passed this way.

Felix Walker was much interested in the Indian symbols painted on the rocks. There were crude figures and mysterious squiggles and lines, some red, others black. Cutbirth told him that war parties passing through the gap would stop to tell of their victory or defeat, how many were killed, and so on. Sometimes a chief would leave his own personal sign.

Did war parties use this gap often? Cutbirth nodded. Now perhaps Boone would post guards at night, Walker suggested. Cutbirth doubted it. Walker and the other North Carolinians had been uneasy about Indians from the first and wanted guards at each nightly campsite. Boone said anyone who would volunteer to stay awake at night was welcome to the task. Guard duty was too much to ask of men who worked such long, hard days. Besides, a good woodsman could tell when Indians were around in a dozen ways. Guarding at night was a waste of time.

The other woodsmen had echoed these sentiments and teased the young men about their worries. Rather than be scoffed at, they had stayed the night through in their blankets, usually so tired from the ax work that they slept unconcerned. Still Walker worried.

Now at Boone's pleadings, the men gathered together and pushed on, following the well-used Warrior's Path, widening it only in a few needed places. The following day they swam their horses across the swollen Cumberland River, rafted their possessions across, and then camped for the night to dry out.

They had come about a hundred miles, Boone told them. There were that many more miles to cover. He suggested all go to bed early and get plenty of sleep. Wasn't Boone posting guards this near the Warrior's Path, Walker asked. Boone shrugged. He anticipated no danger from the red men. He rolled up his tattered blanket with his feet to the fire and soon was snoring. The others followed.

They left the Warrior's Path at the Cumberland River ford. It went directly north to the Shawnee towns along the Ohio. Now the men followed a winding trail, overgrown in places and obscured in others, which Boone referred to as the Hunter's Path. Several days after leaving the Cumberland with hundreds of trees felled and miles of cleared brush behind them, the tired axmen were halted by their leader. They were leaving this path, he told them. It continued in its haphazard way northward to the falls of the Ohio River. It was the route he and Stoner had taken during Dunmore's War to warn the Virginia surveyors. It went through fine land, but not as fine as the place where they were headed. Boone had picked out a big buffalo lick, where all manner of game abounded and the soil was wonderfully fertile, for the site of the first Transylvania Company's settlement. He was sure they, as well as Henderson, would be pleased with the location. Since there was no path whatsoever in that direction, they would really have to work now. However, it would be worth it.

Boone led the way. The cane was the thickest they had ever seen, the laurel old and twisty, and the rest of the growth scrubby and tough. Even hard, calloused hands developed blisters from the axwork, and experienced as they were, they still suffered many gashes on legs and feet when axes glanced from hard timber. Trees rotten at their heart fell the wrong way, and all marveled that there were not more injuries than there were. Boone kept encouraging them, and he kept them well supplied with game. Walker remembered in his narrative an excellent supper of a fine bear. March bears, after a winter's hibernation, were usually poor fare, but the master hunter, Daniel, had provided the best for his men.

One day one of the axmen called out in surprise. Before cutting down a hollow sycamore, he had glanced inside and found a man's skeleton. The men gathered around the tree as Boone examined the bones. The left arm was broken, and the bone was discolored from a bullet. There were no other broken bones, nor any indication on the skull that the man had been scalped. No rifle was found, but there was a powder horn with a brass band around it under the pile of bones. Boone cried out on finding it. He had recognized the horn even before he showed the men the initials on it—J.S.—John Stuart. Stuart had been Daniel's brother-in-law and his companion on his 1769 hunt into Kentucke. One day he had decided to hunt by himself. He left Boone and mysteriously disappeared. Though Daniel searched for him, there had been no trace of the other hunter. Now the lost was found.

The twenty-fourth of March had been an unusually difficult day. The men had seemed to spend more time sharpening their axes than using them. A packhorse had bucked against a tree, bursting open a sack of seed corn and scattering it about. The trailmakers collected what they could of the corn and inched on. The sky filled with murky clouds and the temperature went down. They camped, tired and cold, where the woods were open and where flowed a spring whose banks were blanketed with anemones, trilliums, and trout lillies. They were cheered by Boone's telling them that there were only about fifteen more miles to go.

Huge fires were built and supper cooked. Talk was scanty. Most of the men turned in right after eating. A wind arose and mourned wildly in the trees, but shortly died away. Once in the night, Twitty's bulldog growled and snuffled about, but the captain took it under the cover with him, and it quieted.

The first war whoop awakened the men. It was a blood-chilling sound, shrill, but as loud as a cannon boom in the quiet predawn, and it jerked the axmen straight up out of their beds. There were shots and more whoops. Boone shouted for the men to scatter. He kicked over a pot of stew to put out the glowing embers of one fire, but still there was a reddish glow among the trees from others. With his bullets and gun, he took to the nearest tree.

Squire grabbed his gun and his pouch and horn and rolled into the nearest bush. The pouch and horn turned out to be his jacket. He put it on, for he had forgotten his breeches. He fired at an Indian, then went crawling off to find someone with shot and powder.

There was not too much shooting now, for it was difficult to tell who was who. But there was much thrashing about in the brush as white and red tangled hand-to-hand. Two of the North Carolina youths were helping Felix

Walker off through the woods, for he was wounded and bleeding.

Captain Twitty, sleeping a little apart from the others, had leaped up at the first shout and calmly picked up his rifle. He stood there on his blanket peering into the darkness, the bulldog at his feet baying a deep-throated war cry of his own. Shots began to whistle about the captain, and suddenly he fell, shot through both knees. An Indian leaped from the blackness with a scalping knife gripped in his hand. The bulldog jumped forward, and the brave screamed as its jaws clamped into his flesh. Another warrior rushed up and drove a tomahawk into the dog's brain and then dragged the bitten Indian away.

It was suddenly quiet. The Indians had departed. Boone called together the scattered group. Captain Twitty's colored servant was dead. There were a few minor injuries, but Walker and Twitty were so badly wounded that further travel was impossible. Boone set the men to making a hasty log fort under Squire's supervision, while he and Stoner took off on the trail of the savages. Cutbirth and Jennings scouted the woods for any remaining red men.

The fort built and the two wounded men tended to, the remaining travelers sat with their rifles in their hands, some scared and worried, the others restless and thoughtful. Walker recorded in his narrative that the skirmish had "cast a deep gloom of melancholy" on the company. Paradise contained a red serpent. Was a new land, however rich and promising, worth a man's life?

5

Kentucke—Point of No Return

Daniel Boone finally did get his men to the big buffalo lick that he had chosen as an ideal site for a fort—that is, all those who were willing to continue on with him. A few of the axmen left for their homes in the East. Sudden Indian attacks at dawn were more than these adventurers cared to face. It was better to go back to civilization, where the plow and the hoe were less exciting but certainly safer.

Before Boone left the rude fort his men had built, he buried Twitty, who had died of his many wounds. The captain was placed in the ground beside his colored servant, killed early in the skirmish. And perhaps Boone saw fit to bury with Twitty his bulldog, faithful to the last, guarding its master even in death. Felix Walker could not walk. A sling was made in which to carry him supported between two horses.

Daniel was not so busy with his men's welfare that he forgot his employer. He wrote a letter to Richard Henderson and dispatched it by a horseman. He told of their skirmish and of other Indian attacks on groups nearby. In his letter he pleaded with Henderson to come on, not to turn back because of the Indians, for now was the time to settle and hold Kentucke once and forevermore.

There is only one chance for paradise. Boone realized this. After years of trying to find the meadowlands of Kentucke and failing, he had had to depend on an Indian trader, his friend, John Findley, to lead him there in 1769. Daniel found it all that rumors and stories proclaimed it to be. And he had advised Henderson it was well worth buying.

Boone had brought his axmen almost two hundred miles through the wilderness in fifteen days, cutting a swathe through the woods wide enough for a wagon. The route from Moccasin Gap to the Clinch River, though known as a possible passage during Dunmore's War but infrequently used, he had made into a usable trail. When he turned from the Hunter's Path in Kentucky northward toward his buffalo lick, he had to make an entirely new route. Their average rate of about twelve miles a day meant hard, fast axwork.

Now on the Kentucky River, Boone was to begin a fort, later called appropriately Boonesborough, which Henderson, on his arrival in the middle of April, declared was in an impractical location. He moved the fort to a more easily defended position.

The route to Boonesborough was never to be much traveled. Most immigrants shunned Boone's trail and passed on northwestward along an old Indian trail toward Logan's Station and Harrodsburg, and that path became the Wilderness Road. Boone's wagon road proved too rough for wheeled vehicles. Henderson with great difficulty had managed to get his wagon almost to Cumberland

Gap, but the effort had been too much, and he abandoned it there. It would be a long time before wagons could easily travel the Wilderness Road.

Though Boone met many disappointments and difficulties in his later life, he won everlasting fame as the frontiersman supreme—the first and greatest of buckskinned heroes in the border warfare between Indians and Americans.

In the spring of 1775, Boone and his followers were only a small number of the many people scattered across Kentucke—settlers and surveyors, sightseers and landlookers, simple and typical pioneers all. There was not a hero in sight. It would take the savage redskins to produce an heroic era in the Dark and Bloody Ground of Kentucke.

Had these pioneers brought enough lore and skill with them across the mountains over the Wilderness Road to resist the Indians? Had they acquired enough woodsy know-how over the decades of living on the outer western fringe of the colonies to wrest Kentucke from the wilderness and hold it?

The Kentucky pioneers had the long rifle. Now it was such a constant companion with menfolks that their wives complained the weapon received more and better attention than they did. Certainly men began to give their rifles pet names. Boone had Tick-licker, and it was his favorite gun. He never bragged about the prowess of his rifle or his marksmanship. If asked, he would say he heard Tick-licker speak, and he saw an Indian fall from a log a great way off. This is understatement, which is later to be the basis for many of the humorous tales and much of the literature emerging from this Old Southwest country, a casual way to tell the truth without bragging about it.

There were many tales told, however, by windy and proud persons about their long, slim, deadly guns. One man claimed his rifle could girdle a white oak, nick the skin of a mosquito, knock the topknot off an Indian brave, bring down a flock of turkeys from the treetops, split enough boards to cover a cabin roof, and plow a straight furrow of ground. Another claimed his rifle was so eager to shoot game that it went off half-cocked at the gobble of a turkey.

Although these claims were exaggerated, newcomers to Kentucke were the best of shots. When the Indian ceased to use his bow and arrow, he lost his supremacy in fire power. A warrior could get off six or seven arrows to every one, perhaps two, rifle shots the pioneers could manage. Now the red man with his mediocre trade gun, which he could not repair himself, was in an inferior situation in fighting the frontiersman holed up behind his wooded palisades. His accuracy and rate of fire were much lower than those of the white man.

And the ax—that necessary pioneer tool. Boys, also girls, learned early to handle it, and by the time they were grown, they were quite expert in its use. Axes varied according to the individual's taste—some liked a heavier head, others a shorter handle. Many frontiersmen made their own, though most went to a skilled blacksmith. An ax head was made by folding over a flat piece of red-hot iron to grip a strip of steel, which would serve as the cutting edge. The steel and iron were welded together, and a handle was inserted between the iron folds. The poll, or back end of the ax, was thick and flat, and it weighed more than the bit, the cutting edge of steel. The poll was heavier so as to give a balance and a momentum to the ax's swing. This was an American ax, a new-world ax to attack the thick tree trunks in the great forests of eastern America. It chipped its way steadily westward.

Besides the rifle and ax, the frontiersman had much else to help him in the new land of Kentucke. He knew a wide variety of plants and how to use them to make medicines, teas, dyes, or flavorings. He had the Swedish log cabin, which he could use as a single blockhouse or incorporate into a picket fence to make a stockaded fort, as well as a dwelling place between Indian attacks.

From German settlers he had picked up improved farming methods, from the Scots the art of making whiskey, and from the Indian he had learned the uses of corn, skin clothes, and shoes, the dugout canoe, and a forest fighting style. He had a raggle-taggle bag of superstitions, songs, sayings, and folkways. All these things he brought with him over the Wilderness Road. It was his cultural baggage, and it was to help him hold and shape the first state west of the Appalachian Mountains.

But one thing he once had was his no longer. He left behind forever the thought of turning back. For these men and women, the Eastern coast, England, or Europe no longer existed. They had to go forward into the wilderness, for there was no other way to go. The idea of returning to towns, even to previously cultivated fields and farms, was one that for the most part they simply could not comprehend. They were people trained and determined to live in new and unsettled land, and they could not imagine things otherwise. They had reached the point of no return.

They cut their few ties with civilization without regret. They looked forward to the hard future without undue fear. Sickness, wild animals, and the Indians offered inevitable danger and hardship, no more to be avoided than the coming of storms and winter cold. No use worrying over what cannot be cured and so must be endured. For a man like Daniel Boone, bringing his family to live the perilous life of the wilderness was as natural as the sun rising—there just wasn't any other way.

NEWSCAST OF 1783

The American Revolution ends, and the
United States is recognized as an independent nation,
but for Kentucke there is
more of the same Indian warfare.

DIE-HARD BRITISH AND INDIANS FIGHT ON

By 1783 the Revolutionary War has been over for two
years, but the treaty negotiations are still going on in
Paris, France. There is much argument over the boundaries of the United States. Rumors are that the Mississippi River will be the westernmost one, while the
Great Lakes will serve as the northern limit.

Kentuckians are not much concerned over the boundaries as the year gets under way. They still have an Indian
problem to deal with. The many tribes north of the Ohio
River say that they will refuse to accept the terms of the
peace treaty that gives away their lands. They believe
Great Britain, their former ally, has no right to cede
land on which red men are still living and which the
Americans did not conquer during the war.

That means more raids across the Ohio, more am-
bushes, horse stealing, and dawn attacks. And the Kentuckians feel certain the British are still supplying the Indians with guns and bullets. The British are retaining
their main forts at Niagara, Detroit, and Michilimacki-
nac, though these military-trading posts are supposed to

be relinquished so as to be turned over to the United States.

Kentuckians learned long ago that a line drawn on a map or listed in a treaty could not stop them. Boundaries are to be crossed when the time comes to do so. The Indian menace will be difficult to stop unless drastic action is taken.

Will the United States government do anything? Many believe not, for it is yet too weak to handle such a problem. Virginia might give some aid, but the Kentuckians realize that once again their survival will depend mostly on themselves and their own resources.

CIVILIZATION CREEPS ACROSS KENTUCKE

March, 1783, finds the three Virginia counties in Kentucke organized into one judicial district. A log court and jail is to be built at Danville. This is fine for punishing white law breakers, but useless against Indian war parties. Northern Indians are reported visiting the southern tribes to try to get them to battle the Kentucke settlers.

Although worried at such reports, the frontiersmen are diverted by talk of horse races and of large sums of money wagered, won, and lost, and also by news of distilleries being built south of the Kentucke River. Horse racing, whiskey making, courthouse and jail—surely civilization is creeping across the Dark and Bloody Ground.

CAPTIVITY LITERATURE

Summer comes with fine crops and more trading activity in the growing towns of Lexington and Louisville and in the smaller settlements around the main forts of Har-

rodsburg, Boonesborough, and Logan's. But the warm
weather also brings more Indian raids against single out-
lying cabins and the ambush of a greater number of travelers.

The Kentuckians learn that in the East people are
reading "captivity literature" and reveling in the sensa-
tionalism of savage cruelty and torture. These are
pamphlets purportedly written by men and women who
were captured by the Indians during the Revolutionary
War, the French and Indian War, or even earlier wars,
such as King Philip's. They tell the story of those who
were captured, of their savage treatment at the hands of
the Indians, of their harrowing escape or rescue, and of
their reunion at long last with their families.

It is ironic to those in Kentucke who are still fighting the red man. If Easterners want the real thing, let
them come west. There are plenty of Kentuckians who
have been captured by Indians and are still living in the
Bloody Ground, risking capture and death again in order
to hold on to Kentucke. And they can't waste time on
either writing or reading pamphlets. These fighting frontiersmen are talking among themselves about breaking
away from Virginia and forming a separate state and
managing their own affairs.

East and West are threatening to split apart. What
would this separation mean to the young United States?

JOHN FILSON ARRIVES IN KENTUCKE

In the fall of the year, a steady stream of immigrants
comes into Kentucke. The settlements are growing and
beginning to stretch their muscles. The continued pres-
ence of the British beyond the Ohio River in the North-

west Territory makes them uneasy, and the menace of
Indian war makes them restless. They want any kind of
action, and Virginia's government seems to them over-
slow and cautious. There is more and more talk of cutting away and becoming an independent state. And peti-
tions are being circulated among the settlers to effect this.

There is one immigrant who arrives in October looking
for good land. He is a schoolteacher from Pennsylvania.
He is also a surveyor, and he surveys some of the Ohio
River while boating to Kentucke. His name is John Filson, and he is to have a vital influence on Kentucke's future.

PART FOUR

JOHN FILSON

Booster—Business American

Kentuckians, Trojans, and Greeks

John Filson reined his horse to a stop to watch a boy
spearing fish with a three-pronged gig. The youngster
was wading slowly along the opposite bank, staring into
the water. Suddenly he drew back his arm and threw the
gig. There was a flash of gold in the water as the sun
perch flicked away untouched. The boy grabbed the floating spear and waded on.

Gold in the Kentucke waters. Gold in the Kentucke
land. Was there ever such a place? Last fall when he arrived, John Filson had had great expectations about this
country he had heard so much of back home in Pennsylvania. But it had exceeded his wildest hopes. His imagination had been so fired that he had decided to collect
all the information he could and make it into a guide-
book with a map to accompany it.

He rode on up the slope toward Fort Harrod. A couple of hunters were entering the gate with a dead elk on
a pole between them. A noble beast, the elk, as befitted
Kentucke's natural setting. Everything in this land, from
trees to game to fossil bones, seemed bigger and better
than ordinary.

Filson stopped at the top of the rise to gaze out over

the fields and woods. It was late May, a day shimmering with dancing light and a lazy warmth. Kentucke in any direction he looked—Kentucke where the cold of capricorn did not chill or the scorching heat of cancer burn. He must remember that phrase and insert it in his book.

Turning, Filson sat a moment, taking in the rough picket wall of the fort and the corner blockhouses with their overhanging second story and the empty eyes of the loopholes. Fort Harrod had seen a lot of fighting, as had most of the stockades in Kentucke. He had been teaching school in Pennsylvania then, but he had heard about the fights and skirmishes and chases from the lips of the frontiersmen who were involved. And what battles he had heard about around the cabin hearthstones! As fierce as any in the days of the ancient warriors when the Argonauts roamed and Ulysses and Ajax wielded their weapons. When his book was published, people would read about the Kentuckians as they read about the Trojans and Greeks.

He entered the fort and dismounted, then went searching for James Harrod, but Jim was away trailing some Indians who had stolen several horses, according to his wife, Mrs. Ann Harrod. However, her husband had endorsed Filson's manuscript with his signature, as he had been requested. The teacher unwrapped the manuscript from its waterproof covering. There were the names of three leading citizens of Kentucke who had given him so much information, helped him with his map, and who now recommended both to the public as truthful and accurate. First came Daniel Boon (Filson never used the "e" on Boone), then Levi Todd at whose home near Lexington the author had written most of the book, and now James Harrod, who had laid out the first town in Kentucke. The endorsement of these three would give his work a prestige of authority.

Filson told Mrs. Harrod to thank her husband for his trouble. He would be sure to bring the Harrods a copy of the printed book and map when he returned. He bowed and left. Outside, he took ink horn and goose-feather pen from his saddlebag and wrote above the three men's names: "Witness our hands this 12th day of May, Anno Domini 1784." Except for a few word changes and small insertions, his book was ready for the printer. He must hurry on to Philadelphia.

2

Coming Soon—the
First Happy People

The mileage chart in Filson's book gave the distance from Harrod's Fort to Logan's as fourteen miles. Filson had checked with many Kentuckians about the distances between stations and points along the Wilderness Road and had found little variance in the figures given. Now he had the opportunity to check the mileage as he went for the first time over the road. He timed it by his horse's steady walking gait of four miles an hour.

He stopped at the creek below the fort to let his horse drink. Logan's had two-story blockhouses at three of its corners as did Fort Harrod, though Logan's Fort was smaller. It had been the smallest of the only three forts standing in the Year of the Bloody Sevens, 1777, when the Shawnee and British all but took Kentucke. The riflemen here had dwindled to a mere fifteen then, and it was often touch-and-go as to how long they could hold out against the sieges.

Logan's Fort was a busy place generally. The route from the Cumberland settlements far to the south ended here. Another path came here from the bustling town of Lexington, and of course the road from Louisville ran here after passing Harrod's Fort. Travelers usually stopped at Logan's to form into large groups to go through the wilderness. The more men and guns there were, the better was their chance to avoid Indian attacks and so get through safely to the Blockhouse, a few miles beyond Moccasin Gap and the eastern terminus of the Wilderness Road in Virginia.

Filson headed his mount up the slope among the rotten tree stumps. There were several loaded horses outside the gate and a man watching them. Filson stopped and asked if there was a group leaving for the east. The man went on picking his teeth as if he hadn't heard. Then he took the twig from his mouth and nodded and said it was leaving right away. Filson asked if he might join them. The man looked at his pick, then went back to poking at his gums with it, talking at the same time. They wanted Indian fighters. Was Filson one? He didn't look like much of a fighter. He looked prissy, more like a man of God than a man of the woods. And that musket Filson had tied to his blanket behind his saddle—could he use it?

Well enough, Filson answered. He was a surveyor and a teacher and, he added a little proudly, an author.

The man spat out the twig with disgust. Book learning! It had ruined many a good man. It was no good for farming nor for fighting Indians. He hadn't sent his sons to school, and every one had grown up to be a hard worker, tough as hickory and keen as frog hair. Couldn't a one of them read or write, and they had the best farms in Rowan County, North Carolina. And that's where he was headed back. He should never have left. He should never have sold his acres in Rowan. He hadn't gotten half of what they were worth. He'd come out to Kentucke expecting to get rich and lead a good life.

Instead, he had found land covered with trees, game getting scarce, and Indians behind every bush. He was disgruntled. Who could plow land with a rifle in one hand, watching out for redskins instead of tree roots. Who could stay in a place where bullets flew around every time he went to the spring for a piggin of water?

But then he reckoned a teacher wouldn't understand his troubles. Book learning was easy anywhere. It just wasn't worth what little trouble it took.

Filson didn't say anything. He was used to this, back in Pennsylvania as well as on the frontier. There were men of this type everywhere, he had found, and he never tried to argue with their wrong-headedness. If he went with this group, he would have to listen to the man's yapping all the way, but one was never able to choose one's traveling companions through the wilderness. One took potluck and went on. All in all, it was a good thing this man was leaving Kentucke. People who came hoping to get rich quick, who objected to the dangers and hardships and work, weren't needed. They would never make good citizens when Kentucke became a state. And surely it would do so in a few years.

A woman rode out of the fort and halted beside Filson. She held a child in front of her, and another little girl clung to her waist from behind. She asked if he was joining their party. Filson nodded. She smiled. The more there were, the safer they would all be, she told him.

The man leaning against the wall snorted, saying sneeringly that Filson would add nothing to their safety. He was a learning man, not an Indian fighter. The woman's smile broadened. Good, she said. Perhaps Filson would have time to teach her girls their letters around the camp-fire at night.

The teacher said he would be delighted at the opportunity to enlighten her children. He added that he hoped such a fine woman wasn't leaving the state.

No, never, she answered firmly. She and her husband and children loved Kentucke and hoped to live there always. Unfortunately, Shawnees had killed their cattle and burned their cabin. Her husband had decided to go to the settlement of Castlewood on the Clinch River to buy two cows and some pigs. And it seemed like Providence, for now she had an opportunity to go back to Castlewood and show her two little girls to their grandparents. And wasn't that fine?

Filson smiled. Now here was a real Kentuckian! Then he hurried inside the fort. He wanted to buy a flitch of bacon to take with him. He had cornmeal and some smoked deer meat Levi Todd had given him. But he didn't believe there would be much game to kill along the roadway or a chance to hunt away from the path.

By the time he joined the group, they had all assembled and were ready to leave. Filson looked them over. There were twenty riflemen, four of whom were boys who looked to be about twelve. Of the rest some were on horseback, some walking. There were five packhorses loaded with gear—someone else didn't care for Kentucke and was leaving for the safer East. And one of the horses carried a featherbed over its back, and from each side of the tick, a young head poked out, feathers in their hair but with big grins of delight at traveling in such a soft fashion. The horse was also loaded with a spinning wheel—another one discontented with Kentucke. How sad! A land of such promise and possibility, such hope and excitement, and people left it for the doldrums of the East!

Filson introduced himself to the company and told them he was headed for Philadelphia. The others welcomed him, and the procession began to descend the slope to the Wilderness Road. Filson looked back at the fort from the hollow below. One thin young girl waved from the gateway. Her hair was stringy and her sack-like dress faded, but she waved vigorously. Was she envious of their going back to civilization? Filson hoped not. This country was surely favored with the smiles of heaven and would soon be inhabited by the first happy people the world had ever known.

He waved back and then trotted on to catch up with the others on the Wilderness Road.

3

To Kentucke—the Future!

The group spread out when they reached the wider, more easily traveled Wilderness Road. Filson fell in with a Kentuckian at the rear. He was riding east with two unladen packhorses, and he hoped to bring back powder and lead for Linn's Fort, a few miles south of Louisville. The northern Indians had stepped up their raids lately, and it was rumored the Chickamaugas from the south were going to help ambush travelers along this very roadway. By fall warfare might be as terrible as it was in 1777. Reports had it that the Wataugans had found a vein of lead near their settlement, and the Linn Fort people hoped he would buy some bars of it. As for powder, he had no idea where he was going to get that. But get it he must if Linn's Fort was to stand any sieges.

He had a scarred ear, red and torn and puffy. He told Filson an Indian chief had chewed it into that shape when he and the savage were engaged in hand-to-hand combat. While the Indian was busy chewing on him, the man went on, he was steadily carving open the chief's stomach and taking out folds and folds of his guts. Filson grimaced, and the frontiersman laughed at his squeamishness.

Filson was fascinated with the man, though all he could talk about was fights and deaths and scalping. He had fought side by side with his rifle, "Quick-Shoot," at many different stations across Kentucke, and the two of them had been on raids against the Indian towns. When he told of the skirmishes between Kentuckians and the redskins, blood spurted everywhere, bubbled across the ground, dripped from the trees, and smeared the sky. If there had been that much bloodshed, Filson knew, not a Kentuckian or a northern Indian would be left alive by now. Still the tales helped pass the journey.

The party stopped at the Crab Orchard to drink the various colored sulphur waters and to bottle some of it to carry along for medicinal purposes. Filson had no time to join the water samplers, for the Linn Fort man hustled him off among the thickets of crab-apple trees to seek out the grave of a man who had been flayed alive by Indian squaws, a strip of skin at a time. The two of them and "Quick-Shoot" never did find the burying place and finally gave up. By then the others had departed, and they had to gallop along the roadway to catch up.

The travelers passed English Station without stopping. This was the last fort in Kentucke. Now ahead lay the true wilderness, where the way was rocky, the thickets inhospitable, where the trail wound through the dimness of tall cane and under thick mats of laurel. They camped for the night at the head of Dick's River. The Linn Fort man told Filson the stream was named for a Negro slave killed here by the Indians, that he had come along just after the killing of the colored servant and had helped bury him. Some spelled the name Dix, but that was incorrect.

Filson made his cooking fire a little apart from the

others. While it was starting, he sat down with his back against a log and his manuscript on his lap and began correcting it. He wanted this book as perfect as he could make it. He had collected information and written the book since his arrival last October. And part of that time he was out looking for and surveying his three tracts of land. It had been a hasty job, the more reason he had best scour it now for errors.

Looking up, he found his two little pupils standing in front of him, too shy to speak. He greeted them, and while they sat quietly nudging and pinching each other, he drew the first four letters of the alphabet on a piece of his precious paper and set the little girls to copying them on smooth wood chips with pieces of charred wood for pencils.

Suddenly he noticed his horse had strayed. He had forgotten to hobble it after taking off the saddle. Bidding the little girls continue their task, he set off to look for the animal.

He searched along the creek, stopping to watch the ivory-billed woodcock dig at a rotten tree trunk and take a huge white grub from the wood. He wondered if it really had a pure ivory bill as some of the frontiersmen had told him. Sometimes he hardly knew whether to believe what was told or not. Some things that had seemed to him fantastic, he now knew for a fact to be true.

He went on admiring the blooming haw shrubs and the variety of flowers. He didn't know much about flowers and shrubs, because grammar and ciphering had seemed more important to him. Finding his horse at last, he led it back along the roadway toward camp. Behind him he heard a great commotion, and he turned to find a group of immigrants riding along the trail. They asked what place this was, and when he told them, they wanted to know how far away the next station was. That would be English Station, eight miles westward. They hurried off believing they could make it before candlelight.

However, one young man and woman stayed behind with their packhorse. Did Filson think they could join the company headed back east? They were not going to live in Kentucke, they said. The girl was already missing her kin and friends back in South Carolina. They had met two groups en route here, each of which told them that Indians were still raiding, and it was foolish to stay in such a land, much less try to raise a family. So they wanted to return with Filson's group.

Filson led them back to his campfire, tied his horse near some cane, dismissed the little girls, and asked the woman if she would cook their supper. While she prepared the side meat and journey cakes of cornmeal, he read to her and her husband from his book.

He read of Daniel Boone's roving excursions in Kentucke when it lay empty of settlers. He turned to the pages of curiosities which told of salt, of sulphur and bitumen springs, of underground caves of primeval darkness, of great tusks and teeth of long-dead carnivorous animals, and of strange human skeletons found in curious sepulchres. When their meal was ready, Filson read one last bit: "This fertile region, abounding with all the luxuries of nature, stored with all the principal materials for art and industry, inhabited by virtuous and ingenious citizens, must universally attract the attention of mankind, being situated in the central part of the extensive American empire . . ."

While they ate, the young man asked questions. Filson replied enthusiastically. Riches and happiness lay ahead

for anyone willing to make a few sacrifices now. There
were dangers, yes, as his account of Daniel Boone
showed, but it was worth the risk. Surely this young fellow knew how to use a rifle. As for company for his wife,
these were friendly people living in Kentucke, and since
they would probably have to spend much time close to a
fort, they would very soon make new friends. After all,
it was up to the young people of this country to look
ahead, not back. He urged them to stay, offering them
choice lots on his property east of the Big Bone Lick.

The following morning when Filson and those with
him headed toward the settled East, the young couple
went westward toward their future in Kentucke. Filson
was most pleased. The way for Kentucke to grow was by
attracting immigrants, young people such as these two he
had persuaded to stay here. The more immigrants there
were, the faster towns grew. Helping the public prosperity of this raw new land would in time help the private
prosperity, and he, with his holdings of land, had a private interest in Kentucke, as did Logan, Harrod, Todd,
and other leaders.

John Filson, the oldest in a family of eight children,
had never had much success in business dealings. Instead
of turning to him in times of trouble, the younger ones
looked to the second oldest, Robert, who was prosper-
ing in Pennsylvania. Robert never chided his older
brother, yet John must have felt guilty about his many
failures, for he was always writing Robert about his pro-
spective plans. He had high hopes for the new land of
Kentucke. However, very few of John's schemes proved
profitable, and in the long run Robert bore the brunt of
John's search for wealth.

4

Troubles on the
Wilderness Road

The second day of travel, after the young people had left them, proved to be one of those days of troublesome happenings. At the first creek they reached after breaking camp, one of Filson's little pupils decided to cross on a fallen log lying over the stream near the fording place. Halfway over on this raccoon bridge, she slipped from the log into deep swiftly-moving water. Her screams brought her father running, and he soon pulled her out, coughing and spluttering. She rode quietly behind her mother the rest of the morning.

Then one of the men on foot sat down on a stone to retie his moccasin and a copperhead bit him, striking him fully in the calf of the leg. The man sprang up, shouting, and killed the snake with his hatchet. He bled his wound and bandaged it with plantain and kept walking, refusing offers of a ride. But by midmorning his leg was much too swollen to stand on, and he had to give up. The Linn Fort man lent him a horse.

Even Filson had his mishaps. Cutting himself a piece of smoked jerk, he dropped his knife in the mud. Though he searched for half an hour, he couldn't find it.

One of the twelve-year-old boys killed a deer that

charged out of the woods at him. It was a quick shot, and he was pleased at having gotten his supper so easily. But the deer was thin and diseased, and he left it where it fell.

As the party forded the Rockcastle River, the bundles on a horse came untied, and woolen socks, dresses, and a brass-button waistcoat went floating off. It took some time to retrieve the clothes. They finally continued on the roadway and pushed steadily ahead. By afternoon they had passed the thicket of hazel trees known as Hazel Patch and reached the turnoff to Boonesborough. It was darkening, but as they were making good time, they kept going.

At Raccoon Creek the Linn Fort man showed Filson the grave of a family who had died the year before. They had camped in a fork of the creek. During the night the creek rose and cut them off. The man drowned; the mother and children perished from cold and exposure. The Linn Fort man said they were the only deaths he knew of along the Wilderness Road that were not caused by Indians.

Here a sudden swarm of gnats and midges settled on the head of one of the horses, causing it to rear and buck and throw its woman rider to the ground. Then it charged through the woods smashing into trees and bushes. Filson and the men chased it, while the women tended to the fallen rider's cuts and scratches.

By twilight the horse had not been found, and the travelers decided to camp there for the night and search for it the following morning. One of the men returned with the news that he had found where Indians had stayed, and the ashes of their fire were still warm. This made the

wayfarers most uneasy. Though they had posted guards
the night before, tonight they doubled them. The men
drew lots for guard duty. Filson got the first shift, which
lasted till midnight.

As he was loading his musket, his friend from Linn
Fort said he needed something better than that. He offered to lend Filson "Quick-Shoot," but the teacher knew
he wasn't serious. Few frontiersmen were ever willing
to lend their favorite weapons. The man who hated edu-
cation remarked to the travelers near him something
about how safe they would be with Filson on guard,
for he could throw a heavy book or call out big words if
the Indians attacked. Filson didn't catch all of his re-
marks, but several around the campfires laughed uproariously. Filson shrugged and took his post by a spring
at the edge of their camping place.

He didn't mind guard duty. It gave him a chance to be
away from the others and to make plans for the future
uninterrupted. On his return to Kentucke, he must find settlers to buy his land. Perhaps he could lay out a town on
one of his three tracts. There was a bank of fine clay
along one of his creeks. He could build a kiln there and
bring in a potter to make dining ware.

An owl sounded overhead, and behind him Filson
heard tiny feet scurrying through the leaves. Two wolves
called back and forth to each other. At least they
sounded like wolves to Filson. Yet they might be Indians. They often used animal calls to signal to each other.
He stood and stretched his cramped muscles. The howls
and cries continued. As the teacher picked up his musket,
he heard someone approaching through the woods. He

tensed, waiting. Now it sounded more like two people coming toward him.

He backed against the tree. Should he call for help or shout at the intruders? The footsteps were close now, and Filson decided it was time for action. He shouted that the redskins were here, aimed his gun into the darkness, and fired.

The camp came alive at once. Children screamed and ran this way and that. Men shouted orders, but in the noise and confusion none could be heard. Filson was trying to reload his musket in the dark but couldn't. He moved back toward the nearest fire to see better.

And out of the darkness walked a horse. It stood there with its head lowered, its eyes gleaming in the firelight. The Linn Fort man pulled up beside Filson. He looked at the horse and then at the teacher and began to laugh. Others came running up, and he told them that one four-legged Indian had attacked the camp but had been captured by Filson. The teacher joined in the laughter. He was quite relieved that it wasn't an Indian attack. The horse was the animal they had searched for. Its owner came up and led it away, and the camp settled back to sleep. But every once in a while there was a guffaw from a blanket or a tent, and Filson knew who was being laughed at.

They were up before light the following morning and off down the Wilderness Road by dawn. They traveled hard all that day and by nightfall had reached the banks of the Cumberland River. They camped at the edge of a canebrake and spent the night in peace and quiet.

The following morning they forded the Cumberland

in shallow water, crossing on a gravel bar that slanted across the stream. Climbing the bank, they kept on, knowing Cumberland Gap lay not too far ahead. In the shadow of Pine Mountain, they found three bodies by the road, dead and mutilated, only recently killed. The faces of the man, woman, and little boy were slashed and cut, and the top of each head was missing.

The party was upset and anxious to leave the scene. Filson tried to borrow a shovel to dig a grave, for it was only right to give them a Christian burial. But the others went on in a hurry, ignoring Filson's request. This was the reason they had left Kentucke, some of them said. They didn't want to end their lives in this fashion. The savages might still be lurking about. They would not risk their lives to bury strangers. All that mattered was to get safely away as quickly as possible.

In the end Filson and the Fort Linn pioneer stayed and piled stones over the bodies. With a slate crayon Filson printed on one of the rocks that an unknown family killed by Indians lay there. Then the two men followed after the others.

Where the path that Elisha Wallen and his men followed through Hunter's Valley merged with the Wilder-Road, Filson's pupils bid him fare-thee-well. He had taught them their letters, and they gravely shook his hand in thanks. Then the girls and their parents rode off up Hunter's Valley toward Castlewood, not too far distant.

The others continued eastward and later that day arrived at the Blockhouse. In seven days they had traveled the wilderness, fording numerous creeks and rivers, climbing Cumberland Mountain, Wallen Ridge, and Powell Mountain and putting up with the mishaps and inconveniences that were the pioneer traveler's lot. They had traveled with fear and so had pushed themselves hard. Seven days for two hundred miles of rough road was a better than average time for a mixed group such as this one Filson went with.

The Blockhouse was a log building of two floors with the upper story extending a few feet out over the lower on all sides. It was erected in 1777 by John Anderson seven miles east of Moccasin Gap and about the same distance north of Long Island in the Holston River. Trails from Pennsylvania, eastern Virginia, and North Carolina converged here, making it a logical starting point for the Wilderness Road. Many immigrants waited at the Blockhouse till a group formed large enough to offer a threat to attacking Indians, then headed west.

John Filson bid the Linn Fort frontiersman good-by and promised to look him up on his return to Kentucke. Waving a farewell to his other traveling companions, he rode his solitary way northward up the Great Valley of Virginia toward a future he hoped would bring him wealth and happiness.

Wilderness Road
Invention Completed

On October 22, 1784, a Pennsylvania paper carried an advertisement for a book published that very day. It was *The Discovery, Settlement and Present State of Kentucke* by John Filson, and the book was illustrated by a map drawn from actual observations by that same man. The price was a dollar and a half, and several places were listed as offering the book and map for sale.

With this publication the invention of the Wilderness Road was completed. The parts of the map that Walker and Wallen and Boone had contributed were connected and incorporated on Filson's printed page, where place names moved mile by mile in columns from the Blockhouse to Logan's Fort. The Wilderness Road, which wound tortuously across mountains and through streams, where bloodshed, death, and danger lurked and were to continue to lurk for another decade, this road Filson reduced to a handful of names and black-lined miles seemingly as easily traveled as moving a finger from one name to another. The author never called it Wilderness Road or even Boone's Road. On his map he designated it as "The Road from the Old Settlements in Virginia to Kentucke thro' the great Wilderness." In his book it became a small part of the "Road from Philadelphia to the Falls of the Ohio by land," a total distance of 826 miles. But Filson had good reasons for extending the Wilderness Road eastward as well as to the west. In his preface he states that his book is a "compleat guide" for those who wish to travel to Kentucke, that he wrote not from lucrative motives but to inform the world about the "happy climate and favorable soil" of Kentucke. Nevertheless, he was nowhere nearly as disinterested as he claimed. His book is what is called promotional literature. Filson was advertising the new land of Kentucke in the most optimistic and favorable terms. Whatever is good in Kentucke is mentioned, but anything that would be unfavorable is ignored or minimized.

Filson was a booster for Kentucke. A book and a map were one sure way to gain attention for that western land. He knew that Philadelphia was a port of entry for foreigners. Ambitious and hard-working newcomers were an asset to any attempt to open up the wilderness, and he desired them for Kentucke. So Filson began his mileage chart at Philadelphia, and he ended it at Louisville, where those who came to Kentucke by water usually disembarked. Why have a mere two hundred miles of Wilderness Road when one four times as long would be much more useful? As long as all roads led to Kentucke, it made small difference where they began.

There had been promotional tracts before Filson's. America must have been helped in its settlement by such works, for almost every British colony along the Atlantic seaboard had at one time or another glorified its attractions in an effort to lure men and money. Certainly there would be many more such books and pamphlets advertising the new towns and states as Americans moved west and boosters attempted to attract people to their own particular localities.

John Filson hoped to begin his personal prosperity in Kentucke. His teaching life in Pennsylvania and Delaware had brought him little in dollars or respect. In this new country he had claimed over twelve thousand acres of land. If Kentucke progressed, surely he would be part of that progress. Also he and a friend had entered a claim that they believed included a long-lost silver mine. One John Swift was rumored to have found a silver mine in a remote valley of the Cumberland Mountains and cached a great quantity of ore there. Kentuckians speculated and worried over its existence for years. James Harrod, the founder of the first settlement in Kentucke, disappeared in 1792, supposedly seeking the mine. Filson's claim came to nothing. No silver mine has ever been found in the eastern mountains of Kentucky, but then and now it was a source of exciting rumors and romantic tales.

Filson was one of those Americans to whom material wealth and what it could command were all important, a breed that was not new upon the planet, but one that in this new country attained great numbers with fresh energy and vitality. The term businessman had not come into use yet, and when it would, it carried the meaning of a man who mixed his private business with that of the community in which he lived. Whatever helped his town or state helped him, and vice versa. This businessman, this booster, was necessary to the growth of America. Filson was a businessman, and though he must have gen-

uinely loved and been proud of Kentucke, his principal
hope for it was that it would make him rich and famous.

Pursuing this end, he was in and out of the territory
several times in the years following the publication of his
book. He proposed starting a seminary, he wanted to
write a book about the Illinois country, he studied medi-
cine, and with two partners he set about laying out a
town on the Licking River in Ohio. He named it Losanti-
ville: L for Licking River; os, Latin for mouth; anti,
Greek for opposite; and ville, French for city. Losanti-
ville was the city opposite the mouth of Licking River,
but it soon became Cincinnati, although Filson probably
didn't know his pedantic name was cast aside. He was
killed by Indians soon after his arrival there. No one saw
him die, his remains were never found, but his partners
said the savages got him. It was very mysterious.

John Filson was thwarted in his ambition to be rich.
After his death, his brother discovered he had left behind only debts, faulty land claims, and empty promises.
But he became famous, though even there it was for the
most part reflected glory, for readers of his book were
captivated by his portrait and memoir of Daniel Boone.
Out of those pages came, larger than life, the hero in
buckskins who was to be a demigod to Americans from
then till now. He was the intrepid, cunning, sharp-
shooting, independent, self-reliant, determined, and resourceful ideal, and his image still looms over the horizon of the American imagination.

Just as Filson had turned Kentucke into a paradise, he
turned Boone into a legend. Both were fine propaganda
devices and served to entice settlers to Kentucke, along
with the map. Especially the map, for the map offered

concrete evidence to irresolute travelers that Kentucke really existed, that there was a way in and, if need be, a way out, that others had followed this path and that it could be followed again. The map was a sign and a talisman. And more and more immigrants came.

And all that travel, of course, was what was needed to make all those places that had been explored and marked by various people at different times and for particular purposes merge into one roadway.

The dictionary implies that one can discover only something that is already there, as Columbus "discovered" America. But the Wilderness Road was invented, for it came into being where nothing had previously existed.

And in the process of inventing it, the English Colonials had become Americans.

THE INVENTION OF THE OLD
WILDERNESS ROAD

(from the Blockhouse, Virginia, to Logan's Fort,
Kentucky)

Here are the various sections of the Wilderness Road as
contributed by the four pioneer travelers who brought the
roadway into being:

THOMAS WALKER: Cumberland Gap; also the section of the road from that gap to the Cumberland River.

ELISHA WALLEN : the route from the Clinch River to Cumberland Gap (this much is known—how much more of the Wilderness Road he used cannot be stated definitely).

DANIEL BOONE: the section of the Wilderness Road from Moccasin Gap to the Clinch River; also a strip of the road from the Cumberland River to a few miles beyond present-day London, Kentucky.

JOHN FILSON: the section of the road from the Blockhouse, Virginia, to Moccasin Gap; also from a few miles beyond present-day London, Kentucky, westward to Logan's Fort.

EPILOGUE

For many years the Wilderness Road continued to be a well-traveled thoroughfare. But it continued to be dangerous until the Indians north of the Ohio River were finally defeated in 1794 by Mad Anthony Wayne at the Battle of Fallen Timbers. The same year Kentuckians and Tennesseans teamed together to crush the Chickamauga Indians along the Tennessee River. The road was then safe from savages, but it needed improvement if wagons were to reach Kentucky over it. These were made, but it was too late. Immigrants were now searching for rich land in the newly opened Ohio country and the territory west of it. Many were following Boone's example and crossing the Mississippi to settle in the Missouri territory.

Today the general route of the Wilderness Road through western Virginia and into Kentucky has been designated the Daniel Boone Highway, and the D.A.R. have placed many markers along it. Cumberland Gap is a National Historical Park, and the spot where Doctor Walker built the first log cabin in Kentucky is a state park. Most of the old Wilderness Road lies buried beneath farms and shopping centers, asphalt and town squares.

Yet it served a great purpose. It led the pioneers over the mountain barrier and into the heart of the land that was eventually to become theirs, a nation of Europeans rather than a handful of Indian tribes, and a first experiment in that curious new form of government—democracy.

A road is not like a river. A river has a definite beginning, in headwaters, springs, and brooks, and a definite terminus perhaps in a larger river but eventually in an ocean.

A road begins where the traveler gets on and ends where he gets off. The path on which the British colonists set foot still winds ahead of us. Along its meanderings the new-world settlers became Americans. What Americans will yet become depends on what they expect of the territory ahead, how well they read the signs, and how keenly they remember the country that they have already traversed.

BIBLIOGRAPHICAL ESSAY

The material in this book has been gleaned from a wide number of sources, a sentence here, an idea there, facts everywhere. It would serve no purpose to list even a part of such a long list. However, for those interested in more information about the four people in this book and the road itself, the following are given.

THE ROAD

KINCAID, ROBERT L. *Wilderness Road*. Indianapolis: Bobbs-Merrill Co., 1947.
A very readable book that covers the main happenings along the road from the late 1600's to 1943. Kincaid's Wilderness Road begins in the Great Valley of Virginia and ends at Louisville.

PUSEY, WILLIAM ALLEN. *The Wilderness Road to Kentucky*. New York: George H. Doran Co., 1921.
The author followed the old road by foot and car in the early 1900's, locating its landmarks. This is the most accurate and detailed work on the road itself.

THOMAS WALKER

ABERNETHY, THOMAS P. "Walker, Thomas." *Dictionary of American Biography*. New York: Charles Scribner's Sons, 1936, Vol. XIX, pp. 360-361.

JOHNSTON, J. STODDARD. *First Exploration of Kentucky*. Louisville: John P. Morton & Co., 1898.
This has Walker's journal in full and makes an attempt to locate Walker's actual route.

ELISHA WALLEN

HAYWOOD, JOHN. *Civil and Political History of the State of Tennessee from Its Earliest Settlement Up to the Year 1796*. Nashville: Dallas and Richmond, 1915.
Haywood interviewed pioneers before writing his history. It is not always accurate, but it has the most material on Wallen's long hunts.

REDD, JOHN. "Reminiscences of Western Virginia, 1770–1790," *Virginia Historical Magazine*, Vol. VII, pages 242–253.
Redd tells of long hunters and has a short piece on Wallen, whom he lived near in Virginia.

DANIEL BOONE

BAKELESS, JOHN. *Daniel Boone, Master of the Wilderness*. New York: William Morrow & Co., 1939.

Though it has some errors, it is the best as well as the most easily procured.

JOHN FILSON

FILSON, JOHN. *The Discovery, Settlement and Present State of Kentucke.* New York: Corinth Books, 1962 (paperback).

WALTON, JOHN. *John Filson of Kentucke.* Lexington: University of Kentucky Press, 1956.
A thoroughly researched biography, using all the scanty material about Filson, his book, and map, with a good reproduction of Filson's map.